# ERASMUS

# ERASMUS

## HANDBOOK OF THE MILITANT CHRISTIAN

*Translated with an introductory essay*

*by John P. Dolan, Ph.D.*

FIDES PUBLISHERS, INC.   •   NOTRE DAME, INDIANA

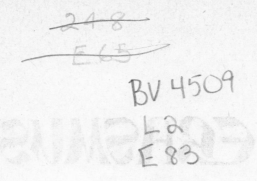

# CONTENTS

NOV 6 1962

# INTRODUCTION

*The Theology of Erasmus and
Christocentric Piety*

# I

Few men have suffered more from having been born before their time than Erasmus of Rotterdam. And yet the world into which he was born gave every evidence of achieving those very conditions of universal peace and tranquillity for which his generation of Christian leaders had striven and hoped. The rediscovery of the world of antiquity had given them a new dimension, a rich and variable source upon which to draw in building a new Christian world. The idea that society and institutions, not merely individuals, could be changed for the better, the conviction that a free unfolding of the human spirit in the framework of a Christocentric philosophy was ushering in a new and marvelous age, was everywhere in evidence among the educated people of Europe. The coincidence of rapid social change with the classical revival at the end of the Middle Ages had produced an aura of optimism which presaged a new era. It was an optimism based on the doctrine of Christ, of which Erasmus wrote: " . . . for what else is this doctrine of Christ which He called a new regeneration, but a restoring or repairing of our nature which in His first creation was good."

It was a time in which men like Erasmus, Colet, and More hoped to spread a new religion of Christian Humanism through-out Europe, a religious humanism that was no mere abstraction confined to the scholar's study, but an attempt to deal with the immediate problems of life and the important problems of the time and thus to make Christianity a more dynamic force in society.

There had been a gradual shifting away from the Augustinian concept of dogma and religion that for centuries had pervaded Western thought. The attempt to divorce religion from material rewards that was the theme of the *City of God* — the conviction that "in God's eyes earthly power and all similar things temporal are not important gifts" — was losing its ancient grip. There was a return to the incarnational view that "Christ by His Incarnation had consecrated the Universe through and through."[1] The attitude that life was nothing more than a pilgrimage, a vale of tears, was giving way to a feeling that a world sanctified by the blood of a God-man was worth improving. The new outlook was a protest against the other-worldliness of the Middle Ages. Human life was felt to be something more than an anteroom for the hereafter. Life here and now must have an undeniable meaning. The revival of an interest in the Greek Fathers, particularly in the Alexandrians, with their deep eschatological concern, fostered the idea of restoration and renewal. Origen, especially, had strongly emphasized the restoration of creational integrity. Through the influence of Platonism, there was a strong belief in the restoration or re-establishment of all men to that spiritual condition possessed by rational nature when there was "no need of eating from the tree of knowledge of good and evil." The bourgeois world which Erasmus wanted to spiritualize was not the least Augustinian in its outlook. As Sellery remarks: "It was not easy for him living in a town which he and his fellows had created and adorned, to regard work as a penalty for sin or this good earth as a place of exile, a vale of tears, as the preacher taught."[2] Homesickness for the other world became more and more rare. There was an interest in life "per se" which the Christian humanist took pains to spiritualize, forming it after Christ. There was an attempt to seek a more spiritualized religion by making the ideals of the Gospel, especially those of the Sermon on the Mount, a living reality.

Like religious reformers of the fifteenth century such as Jean Gerson, Peter D'Ailly, and Nicholas of Cusa, Erasmus had the misfortune of not producing a generation of disciples who could have promulgated his teachings. The *rabies theologorum* of the

---

[1] T. E. Mommsen, "St. Augustine and the Christian Idea of Progress," in *Journal of the History of Ideas*, XII, 763.

[2] G. B. Sellery, *The Renaissance, Its Nature and Origin* (Madison, 1950), p. 18.

sixteenth century had left little place for a man who was to dedicate his life to peace among Christians and who envisioned a Europe united under an enlightened Christian leadership. The breakup of papal Christianity in most of northern and western Europe shifted the emphasis in theology into the realm of polemics and power-politics. The Counter Reformation ushered in an era of confessional absolutism that was the antithesis of all that Erasmus had striven for. His deliberate refusal to form a "third party" to further trouble a confused situation was perhaps the greatest proof of his dedication to peace and tranquillity.

Yet the followers of Erasmus were so numerous and influential that it remains somewhat of a mystery to this day why they did not exert a greater influence. The Erasmians, although they did not form a united front, were represented in almost every court in Europe. The ideas of the great humanist bore weight not so much from the number of those who represented them as by reason of the social and political positions these men held. This varied and influential group included the English Bishop Tunstal, the Archbishop of Culm, John Dantiscus, the Bishops of Augsburg and Basle, the former Bishop of Lund, and the right-hand man of the Emperor, Granvella. The Bishop of Augsburg spoke of Erasmus as his guide to true Christianity and ranked him above the greatest theologians of the past: "Is fuit qui veram pietatis ac religionis viam digito demonstraverit."[3] His ideas on religion, however, were doomed to failure because they were embraced for the most part by ecclesiastical politicians — men whose voices were ignored because they advocated compromise in an age of growing intolerance. The members of few movements in history have suffered a greater disillusionment than the irenicists of the sixteenth century. Recent studies of Seripando, Sadoleto, and Contarini have brought to light again the efforts of these humanistic Cardinals to stem the tide that

---

[3] H. Jedin, *Geschichte des Konzils von Trient* (Freiburg, 1947), p. 294.

was to plunge the Church into a seemingly interminable period of disunity.

Once the Reformation had actually begun, Erasmus had the misfortune of being constantly under attack from Lutherans as well as Catholics. Although he often voiced his determination never to leave the Church of Rome, his refusal to take sides in the religious controversy made him as much a target for the wrath of the curial party as for that of the partisans of Luther. He frankly admitted that he did not have the stuff of martyrs in him. He even feared that he might in the face of crisis deny Christ as did Peter. Yet he hoped that were he ever to face martyrdom he would have the courage to see it through. What man could honestly promise more? What he did not intend to do was to die "pro Lutheri paradoxis." He was opposed to "Erasmians" as much as to Lutherans. He wrote to his friend Coelius Calcagnius, in 1525: "Moreover it is my fate to be pelted by both parties while I try to satisfy both. In your country [Italy] and in Brabant I am considered to be a Lutheran, and in the whole of Germany where I live, so much an anti-Lutheran, that the ardent followers of Luther rave against no one as against me, and they mainly blame me that they do not triumph over the Pope."[4]

If Erasmus was misunderstood by his contemporaries, he had the additional misfortune of faring even worse in succeeding centuries. The Jesuits, particularly Ignatius Loyola, were extremely critical of his spirituality. After reading the *Enchiridion,* Ignatius claimed that it left him cold and dampened his spirit of devotion: ". . . illius libelli lectione refrigescere in se Spiritum Dei."[5] Paul IV, in his frantic attempt to stem the growing success of the Reformation, put all the works of Erasmus on the Index. Yet even St. Peter Canisius admitted that there was no replacement for Erasmus' works on the humanities and that the schools of the society in Germany were in a quandry because

---

[4] P. S. Allen, *Erasmi Epistolae* (Oxford, 1906-1947), VI, 76.
[5] P. Ribadeneira, *Vita Ignatii Loiolae* (Ingolstadt, 1589), p. 49.

of this sweeping legislation.[6] The theologians of Paris and Louvain followed the scholastics of Spain in attacking a man who had reflected in his theology a vision of practical Christianity, based upon a knowledge of the Gospel and the spiritual understanding of a purified heart, instead of on the cold abstractions of the lecture hall.

It was a tragedy that the age of the Enlightenment heralded Erasmus as the precursor of the worshippers of pure reason. The deliberate attempt of philosophers like Montesquieu, Voltaire, and Rousseau to emasculate the writings of Erasmus by extracting the strong Christian element was now added to the biased judgments of the Lutheran and Tridentine divines. Flittner[7] points out that this rationalist view of the great humanist continued throughout the eighteenth and nineteenth centuries. Bossuet, although he could not but admire the literary taste and style of Erasmus, and especially his predilection for the Fathers, nevertheless relegated him to the category of contemporary agnostics. He was culpable because he failed to understand the true nature of scholasticism: "il ignore profondément ce que c'est que la scolastique, et la blâme sans être capable d'en connaître l'utilité."[8]

The notion that Erasmus was all but a freethinker, an earlier Voltaire, finds wide acceptance today. Preserved Smith, representing a liberal Protestant view, holds that in principle at least he was a rationalist. He points out the influence of Valla, "as cold a rationalist as ever was born"[9] and points to Erasmus' interpretation of the Petrine doctrine (Matt. 16:18) as an indication of a nonheterodox position. The use of this scriptural reference to establish proof of papal supremacy is of a rather recent origin. Certainly it was not used during the high point

---

[6] O. Braunsberger, *Beati Petri Canisii Epistolae et Acta* (Freiburg, 1896), II, 49.

[7] A. Flittner, *Erasmus im Urteil seiner Nachwelt* (Tubingen, 1952), p. 150.

[8] Bossuet, *Oeuvres* (Paris, 1845), II, 48.

[9] P. Smith, *Erasmus* (New York, 1926), p. 435.

of medieval papal domination. To merely credit Erasmus with making religion a guide to right living, rather than a doctrine of salvation, is to miss the whole purpose of his tireless efforts to "restore all things in Christ." Troeltsch feels that Erasmus introduced enough of the elements of rationalism into religion to reduce it to a sort of humanitarianism. Yet the departure of Erasmus from traditional *opiniones* and the attempt to evaluate him in term of the *Devotio Moderna* are hardly enough to brand him as a rationalist.

The late nineteenth century, with its interest in critical history, gave some indication of a reappraisal of this great Christian humanist. Lord Acton saw in him not only a precursor of the Reformation but also a man bent upon renovating society through the principle of self-sacrifice. He believed Erasmus was the "greatest figure of the Renaissance. He was the first European who lived in intimacy with another age besides his own."[10] In his later years he lived for the idea that the reform of the Church depended upon a better knowledge of Christianity, "in other words a better self-knowledge which could only result from a slow and prolonged process."[11] Cardinal Gasquet stressed Erasmus' loyalty to the Church in fact as well as in intention. He believed that anyone who examined Erasmus' times could not regard him as either a coward or a crypto-heretic. Though he was "often perhaps injudicious in the manner in which he advocated reform . . . it will commonly be found that his ideas are sound."[12] He mentioned the early attempts to destroy Erasmus' good name by fanatical friars who went so far as to proclaim that his edition of the New Testament was a sign of the Antichrist.

Unfortunately Grisar, although granting greatness to Erasmus as a scholar and controversialist ("his editions of the Fathers

---

[10] Lord Acton, *Lectures in Modern European History* (New York, 1906), p. 89.

[11] Lord Acton, *History of Freedom and other Essays* (London, 1907), p. 58.

[12] F. Gasquet, *The Eve of the Reformation* (London, 1899), pp. 155-156.

are excellent," his treatment of Scripture brilliant, and his *Hyperaspites* "vigorous and triumphant"), nevertheless follows a centuries-old tradition of accusing Erasmus of attempting to reconstruct theology and thereby expose its dogmas to extinction. According to Grisar, Erasmus wished to remain loyal to the Church but his caustic critique so influenced his "idolizing followers" as to render the greatest service to Luther.[13] Grisar's biased and vitriolic attack on Luther, which fills six volumes, gives little attention to Erasmus other than to point out his disagreements with the religious reformer. He miscalculates Erasmus' reform measures in terms of Eck and Emser and evaluates them in terms of post-Tridentine dogmatism. Monsignor Philip Hughes, the English historian, singles Erasmus out for his "unreasoned vindictiveness" and discloses his attitude toward the great humanist by remarking that, in the sixteenth century, "Christendom was not characterized by saints like More and Fisher, but by men like Luther, Zwingli, Professor Erasmus and Cardinal Wolsey."[14] In speaking of Erasmus' controversy with Luther, Hughes writes: "He preferred not to know the great technique that had been built up, and when for example in the controversy with Luther, he came to defend the freedom of the will, his ignorance of the very nature of the problem led him into the most extraordinary blunders."[15]

Christopher Hollis, one of those Catholic writers willing to twist facts for the edification of a partisan reading public, won an American Catholic Book Club award some years ago with his work on Erasmus. Hollis devotes himself mainly to a frontal attack on his subject's character. Finding no evidence that Erasmus ever said Mass, he makes great issue out of this. He insinuates a lack of sincerity in the account by Erasmus of life in the monastery of Steyn. His historiography is at times almost incredible, as when he writes: "Erasmus and Luther both introduced into their controversies habits of overstatement and

---

[13] H. Grisar, *Luther* (St. Louis, 1915), IV, 137-138.
[14] P. Hughes, *The Reformation in England* (London, 1948), I, 123.
[15] *Ibid.*, p. 344.

personal abuse so reckless and unbalanced as to raise considerable doubts of their sanity."[16] He finds the *Enchiridion* a "most improper and irreverent tirading against monasticism." Erasmus' revolt against scholasticism was a revolt "against reason." He finds Erasmus "revolting" — "a person who minimized original sin and taught that men should gratify impulses merely because they are impulses"; — "an irreligious man." One is tempted to say of Hollis what he wrote of Erasmus: "[he] was always a man to prefer perfection of form to accuracy of content, or in other language, that he never told the truth when it happened to be in his interest to tell a lie."[17]

Representative of a large body of contemporary critics of Erasmus, Johan Huizinga, the great Dutch historian, presents another variant of the thesis that Erasmus is basically an ethical humanitarian. He maintains that Erasmus' classicism radically alienated him from traditional Catholicism, and that his sensitive nature was really unable to come to a final determination on the great doctrinal issues of the day. Like many others, Huizinga gives special attention to the unresolved classical-Christian tension in Erasmus: "The foundation of his spiritual life was no longer a unity to Erasmus. It was, on the one hand, a strong desire for an upright, simple, pure and homely belief, the earnest wish to be a good Christian, but it was also the irresistible intellectual need of the good taste, the harmony, the clear and exact expression of the Ancients, the dislike of what was cumbrous and involved."[18] He pays special attention to the negative side of Erasmus' mind when he says: "In spite of his natural piety and his fervent ethical sentiments, he lacked the mystical insight which is the foundation of every creed."[19] For this author Erasmus suffered the Achilles' heel of failing to make decisions. He lacked the depth and the consistency, as well as the fervor, of Luther, Calvin, and Ignatius Loyola. Huizinga mistakes

---

[16] C. Hollis, *Erasmus* (Bruce, 1933), p. 184.

[17] *Ibid.*, p. 20.

[18] J. Huizinga, *Erasmus of Rotterdam* (London, 1952), p. 112.

[19] *Ibid.*, p. 136.

Erasmus' taste for allegory as a trifling aberration, whereas in fact it is one of the clearest testimonies to his debt to the Fathers. Looking upon Luther, Calvin, or Ignatius as representing the only genuinely Christian alternatives of the sixteenth century, Huizinga fails to see the tremendous value of the irenicist of this period who reflected a deep knowledge of the ills of Christendom and whose admonitions, had they been listened to, might have avoided the disastrous split in Christendom.

The French historian Augustine Renaudet, by far the most thorough student of Erasmus and certainly the most penetrating of his critics in the religious sphere, maintains that he is in the first place a humanist, specifically a disciple of the classical moralists, and then a Christian. "De même que son spiritualisme, au fond, procède de Cicéron plus que de Saint Paul, son éthique procède de l'antiquité plus que de l'Evangile."[20] His Christian humanism is

> a humanistic ethic, revised and corrected according to the Gospel. Despite his good intentions, Erasmus is basically untrue to the Catholic tradition with regard to the dogmatic, sacramental and mystical elements in Christianity. His failure to take sides during the early phases of the Reformation is due more to his timidity and temperament than to deep convictions. Rather than make a frontal assault on traditional dogmas and practices, Erasmus wished to disengage therefrom the essential affirmations of Christianity. His lack of understanding of the mystical bases of monasticism led him to judge it to be a useless way of life. Despite his intellectual independence, Erasmus had neither the spirit nor the temperament of an heresiarch.[21]

Again he writes:

> Erasmus knows that human language cannot imprison the infinite; that dogma has developed from the beginning . . . and that this necessary adaptation of dogma to human history is both a development and an enrichment. Such a conception

---

[20] A. Renaudet, *Erasme, sa Pensée Religieuse et son Action, d'après son Correspondance* (Paris, 1926), pp. 13-14.

[21] *Ibid.*, p. 34.

> permits what must be called Erasmian modernism to escape
> the constraint of the Protestant criterion, which posed, in
> principle, in his prefaces of 1516, rejects everything which
> does not seem exactly based upon a primitive text or is not
> in conformity with primitive usage. By it Erasmus accommo-
> dates himself to the provisional shelter offered him by the
> Roman Church.[22]

He directs a great deal of his research to pointing out what he
calls the Erasmian conception of "la troisième Eglise," a Church
that could, of course, be formed only at Rome and with the
approval of the Pope. It would be characterized by evangelical
discipline and respect for Christian liberty. (There was much
to be said for the fear of Erasmus that the fall of Luther would
ruin the evangelical cause and would redouble the tyranny
of the prelates and monks.)

To describe Erasmus as a Modernist, as Renaudet does, is
to make a number of false assumptions. The first is that Catholicism must be understood in its most "retrograde" form. Another is to assume, as so much criticism of Erasmus does, the
defined status of so many of these points of Catholicism during the early sixteenth century. The tendency to evaluate
everything in terms of Tridentine decrees betrays a lack of
historical perspective. Renaudet has recently been criticized,
not only for attempting to interpret Erasmus in terms of modern
Catholic dogma, but for failing to perceive the strong element
of patristic theology in his writings, a blunder that apparently
flows from Renaudet's own lack of knowledge of the Fathers.[23]
The opposition of Erasmus to a useless multiplication of definitions by no means makes him a latitudinarian, for in doing
so he repeats the Fathers, among others St. Athanasius and St.
Basil. Renaudet's criticism of Erasmus for rejecting heresy more
because it disrupts the unity and peace of the Church than
because it is a doctrinal evil can be traced to the ancient work

---

[22] A. Renaudet, "Le Message Humaniste et Chrétien d'Erasme,"
in *Sodalitas Erasmiana*, I (1949), 52.
[23] L. Bouyer, *Autour d'Erasme* (Paris, 1955), p. 155.

by St. Cyprian, *On the Unity of the Church,* which Erasmus edited in 1520.

Albert Hyma, well-known American critic of Erasmus, makes him the precursor of Liberal Christianity. Although Hyma's principal interest lies not so much in Erasmus' theology as in his early life in general and the influence of the *Devotio Moderna,* he does not try to divorce Erasmus' ethical concern from his Christianity.[24] He feels that, like Thomas More, Erasmus was imbued with the medieval ideal of reforming individual Christians. He follows a common trend in describing him as a forerunner of modern Christianity:

> Erasmus spoke in 1515 as hundreds of well-known Churchmen have spoken in the twentieth century. In his opinion it mattered little whether the miracles recorded in the Bible had actually happened or not. As for the doctrines of transubstantiation, or purgatory, and of justification by faith and works, he believed that they might be interpreted in various ways. . . . He said on many occasions that to imitate the life of Jesus was far more important than to argue about dogma. . . . Science meant almost nothing to him. Dogma, on the other hand, meant little more.[25]

In failing to perceive the difference between Erasmus' lack of concern for dogma and the antidogmatism and religious rationalism of the twentieth century, Hyma follows those who assume that the *Devotio Moderna* taught the near-total depravity of man and thus approximated the doctrine of Luther. For Hyma Erasmus' chief significance is that of a critic. He follows Henry Lea in pointing out that Erasmus' gift of ridicule was the most dreaded weapon in the Europe of his time and that he used it mercilessly on the most conspicuous abuses in the Church. In this view, Erasmus found it easy to criticize existing conditions but disliked the work of constructing different ones. If one can read the *Consilium Cujusdam* of 1520

---

[24] Albert Hyma, "Erasmus and the Northern Renaissance," *Medievalia et Humanistica,* VIII, 99-103.

[25] Albert Hyma, *Erasmus and the Humanists* (New York, 1930), pp. 9-11.

and the *Ratio Verae Theologiae* and still contend that Erasmus disliked the work of "constructing new conditions" one's meaning for "constructing new conditions" must be "founding a new church." And there is no doubt that this is something Erasmus had no intention of doing.

As evidence of a changing attitude towards Erasmus on the part of Catholic scholars we might point to the recent work of Louis Bouyer, *Autour d'Erasme*. Stirred no doubt by the writing of Renaudet, Bouyer attempts to refurbish Erasmus and make him acceptable to contemporary Catholicism. Defending him from the charge of latitudinarianism, he writes: "Ethical questions were almost the only ones that interested him. It should be added that they were the only ones for which he felt he had a formation sufficient to permit him to speak of them. But it would be absolutely unjustified to deduce from this that he did not believe in that of which he does not speak."[26] Bouyer exonerates Erasmus in his apparent failure to treat the sacraments by pointing out that a failure to expatiate upon them is not tantamount to a denial. "Whenever Erasmus was backed up against a wall, he categorically accepted, or categorically refused to set aside the authority of customs and canonical prescriptions." Alfons Auer[27] has pointed out quite conclusively that Erasmus was in strict keeping with ecclesiastical tradition in his exposition on the sacraments as signs objectively productive of Christ's grace — "In sacramentis per signa quaedam sensibilia, infunditur insensibilis gratia congruens externis signis symbolum." Erasmus stressed the danger of relying too much on the "ex opere operato" element in the reception of the sacraments which had become the cause of the mechanistic religion of his time: "caro sacramenti non prodest quicquam, sed spiritus est qui vivificat." There is certainly nothing heterodox in pointing out that the mere reception of the sacrament does not confer grace. Erasmus sees this truth most clearly in the

---

[26] L. Bouyer, *op. cit.*, p. 171.
[27] A. Auer, *Die vollkommene Frömigkeit des Christen* (Düsseldorf, 1954), p. 156.

case of the Eucharist. He writes in the *Enchiridion:* "Even if you celebrate Mass daily and live for your own pleasure, not moved in the least by your neighbor's difficulties, as if they had nothing to do with you, you are in the flesh of the sacrament."

Jacques Etienne finds that "spiritualism" is the dominant element in Erasmian theology. There is no question that Neoplatonic elements form a large part of the framework of the spirituality of Erasmus and that this has the effect of leaving in the shadow certain aspects of sacramental efficacy. "The rite is reduced to the role of a pure symbol, thus constituting an inferior level which must be hastily bypassed to attain to reality. For Erasmus the rite is not the means by which and in which I encounter God really and continually, it is but the figuration of this encounter, which I must realize by other means."[28] The other means in this case are the Christocentric dispositions that Erasmus is ever at pains to inculcate by his exhortations:

> His enthusiasm is directed more to the universal assembly of faith and charity than to the hierarchically structured visible organization. This relative devaluation of the hierarchical and sacramental aspects of Catholicism does not at all constitute a betrayal or rejection but a misunderstanding, a disaffection, which is consequent upon his individualistic piety . . . and is understandable enough in a former disciple of the Brethren of the Common Life, where the New Devotion made much more of the soul's contact with the Lord than of enthusiastic involvement in ecclesiastical life.

The *Devotio Moderna* was above all an attempt to approach Almighty God without the burdensome apparatus of late medieval scholasticism. It was also a silent reaction against the accumulated magical and superstitious elements that too often found their way into the popular piety of the time.

It might also be noted that Erasmian spirituality was in many respects deeply influenced by the nominalistic theology of the time. It is only in recent years that there has been a growing

---

[28] J. Etienne, *Spiritualisme Erasmien et Théologien Louvanisten* (Louvain, 1956), p. 14.

realization that this movement profoundly influenced the late Middle Ages. A desire for a recovery of the sense of divine immediacy lay behind it. The overinstitutionalizing of the Church during this period, its deep involvement in the fiscal aspects of a changing economy, and particularly its policy of dispensing the sacraments themselves for a set price, alienated many of the faithful. It might come as a surprise to present-day Catholics that the sacraments at this time were seldom administered without an accompanying stole fee. (In the case of Extreme Unction, for example, the price varied, depending upon the recipient's recovery or nonrecovery.) In the minds of many the sacraments were no longer instruments for increasing participation in divine life, but were mere requirements for graduation into eternal bliss. A quest for immediacy with the divine, independent of the sacramental system, was reflected in the deep current of what Imbart de la Tour terms "evangélisme,"[29] with its heavy Pauline overtones. The fact that St. Paul was converted on his journey to Damascus without the mediation of word and sacrament pointed to a more immediate relationship with God than the established order of sacramental grace. We see this element of Pauline theology deeply rooted in the spirituality of Erasmus, Sadoleto, Contarini and Seripando, the papal legate at Trent.

In Erasmus this individualistic piety was offset by his notion of the universalism of charity and the ideal of the Mystical Body of Christ. As a result of Erasmus' focus on the attitude of the subject toward God, his whole theology is marked by an enthusiastic personalism, and a lively sense of the person is at the base of his reformatory efforts. He is sensitive to religious realities only insofar as they directly concern the individual Christian. For him the goal of theology is not a matter of speculation but, in the words of the *Ratio Verae Theologiae*, "to teach Christ in a pure fashion." Thus in his *De Libero Arbitrio*, Erasmus is

---

[29] Imbart de la Tour, *Les Origines de la Réforme* (Paris, 1948), III, 398.

at his best when describing the experience of freedom, the spiritual attitude by which the sinner confesses his responsibility and attributes to God all that is good in him. Speaking of this personalism, Etienne remarks: "It is precisely in this that Erasmus is a modern; there has always been some attention to the person, but in Erasmus it becomes such a preoccupation that, for him, to put the spiritual subject in parentheses seemed to be infidelity to the object."[30]

Although he risked falling into a vague and dogmatic skepticism, because of his claim that analysis kills the Christian reality, Erasmus' achievement was to see the difference between analysis and living religion. He was cognizant in a very real sense of the difference between dogma and dogmatism. In other words, as most of his critics will agree, Erasmus found the essence of Christian religion to be in the attitude of the individual soul toward its Creator, in short, in *piety*. This piety is fostered by religious exercise, chiefly by meditations on Christ. It is, in short, a humanism of the Cross. Thus, in the *Enchiridion,* he directs the reader to meditate on our Lord's Passion: "the only and chief remedy which of all remedies is of most efficacy and strength against all kinds either of adversity or temptation is the cross of Christ." Genuine piety cannot remain an attitude of mind alone, but must show itself in works of Christian charity.

Since expressions like "consulere pietate" appear with such great frequency in the writings of Erasmus, the central importance of *pietas* for him must be emphasized. We must bear in mind that he looks upon dogmas of the Church almost exclusively as an aid to piety. Writing to his friend John Slechta in 1519, long before the Lutheran affair had reached its later proportions, he says:

> In my opinion, many could be reconciled with the Roman Church, if instead of wishing to fix and define every little detail, we were to let that suffice which is clearly commanded in the Scriptures and is indispensable to salvation. But these things are few in number. Nowadays, however, we make out

---

[30] Etienne, *op. cit.,* p. 20.

of one article six hundred, and some of these are such as could be readily passed over or doubted without any loss of piety. . . . The more we pile up definitions, the more we lay the foundations of controversy, because the nature of mortals is such that when a thing has once been established they cling to it stubbornly.[31]

In his *De Libero Arbitrio* he once again asserts that the simple truths about repentance, the forgiveness of sin, Providence, and ascribing human goodness to God are sufficient for Christian piety. In the same place he inveighs against the sacrilegious curiosity which delves into such questions as whether God knows future contingents; and in the *Ratio* he stigmatizes as useless for piety the minute questions raised concerning the details of Christ's birth.

In the little work, *Liber de Sarcienda Ecclesiae Concordia,* ("On Christian Unity")[32] which he wrote toward the end of his life when the rent in Christendom had gone beyond any real hope of a reunion, he has this to say of the sacrament of Confession:

> The benefit we derive from it depends largely on ourselves. We can choose our own confessor who should be honest and intelligent and to be relied upon to hold his tongue. To him we should confess as freely as we should to God our open and evident faults, and not by our vague and confused words compel him to extract our sins from us. There must be no superstitious repetition, no minute enumeration of all the circumstances, no flying to another priest in case anything has been forgotten at the first attempt. The great thing is to hate our misdeeds and so to order our lives that we commit no mortal sin. He who can do that has no need of confession.

The deprecative element in Confession, the overinsistence on its tribunal nature, with the concomitant shifting of species and endless interrogation, are lamented by many theologians to this day.

---

[31] Allen, *op. cit.,* IV, 113.

[32] For a translation of this, see P. S. Allen, *Erasmus Lectures and Wayfaring Sketches* (Oxford, 1934), pp. 87-94.

Speaking of the Mass, which had become the storm center of the reform movement, Erasmus offers this salutary advice: "There is superstition also in the multiplicity of Masses; the Mass of the Crown of Thorns, the Mass of the Three Nails, the Mass of the Foreskin of Christ, Masses for those who travel by land or by water, for barren women, for women laboring with child, for persons sick with quartan and tertian fevers. Some improvement could be made in these directions."[33] It is interesting to note that this proposal was adopted by the Council of Trent and that most of the liturgical reforms he advocated were eventually introduced. Speaking of the plethora of feast days that had been the target of reform-minded Churchmen for over two centuries, he suggested that they be reduced in number: "There would be no objection to having fewer festivals, if only we keep those that are left with greater devotion." In this proposal he only reiterates what men like Jean Gerson and Peter D'Ailly had proposed at Constance a century before and which were, like many of his other suggestions, put into the legislation of the Tridentine decrees.

For those who accuse Erasmus of neglecting the importance of the sacraments, it might be well to point out that in 1529, seven years before his death, we have his own declaration that he would never dare to leave this life without having confessed his sins to a priest. Just two weeks before his death we have the express testimony of his confessor, John of Breisgau, that he had been to Confession and that his life was one worthy of Christ. "Fuit illi dum viveret aliquities a confessionibus in quo non nisi Christo dignam vitam deprehedebam."[34]

One of the chief grievances of Erasmus was that spirituality had almost been reduced to a matter of status. The laity, particularly, had become something like a spiritual proletariat, an auxiliary body more to be exploited than exhorted. Movements like the *Devotio Moderna* and the numerous confraternities

---

[33] *Erasmi Opera Omnia,* ed. Leclerc (Leiden, 1703-1706), V, 502.
[34] Allen, *op. cit.,* VIII, p. 145.

and brotherhoods of the late medieval period were an indication that the laity were not only dissatisfied with the fiscal abuses associated with the administration of the sacraments but were above all disconcerted with the magical and methodical aspects of accumulated piety, controlled by a not too religiously-minded clergy. In his *Enchiridion* Erasmus attempts to correct this situation by proposing a program of piety that is essentially lay orientated. "Some theologians when treating of the expression 'Church' in the Scriptures take it to mean the priests; and the 'world,' by which is signified evil affections, they take it to mean the laity — as if these did not belong to the Church." In answer to those who say, "I am not a clergyman," or "I am a man of the world," he says, "There are too many who think that the expression 'world' refers only to those who have not embraced the monastic state. In the Gospel, among the Apostles, and for Augustine, Ambrose and Jerome, the expression means the infidel, enemies of the faith and the cross of Christ. It is from this world that Christ separated not only his Apostles but all men who would be worthy of Him."

The overidealizing of monasticism was a special target of Erasmus' criticism. Since the Hildebrandian reform of the early twelfth century there had been periodic attempts on the part of hierocratic theorists of the Middle Ages to remold society to fit the pattern of monastic doctrine and law. As Dom Knowles points out, "The greatest movement of reform aimed, and in part succeeded, in monachizing the Church by putting before clergy and even before laity, monastic discipline and monastic practices and ideals as the universal way of salvation."[35] Pope Paschal II, disciple and successor of Gregory VII, went even further than Gregory in his conception of a new world order. In 1111 he startled his colleagues at Rome by apparently embracing the doctrine of apostolic poverty for the entire Church. The attempt to establish the Church in the world as one vast

---

[35] D. Knowles, *Bulletin of the John Rylands Library,* **XXXIX,** 132.

hermitage was a failure, the ramifications of which were very much alive in the world of the sixteenth century.

The disintegration of monasticism was not entirely unlike the breakup of knighthood. As Huizinga remarks of the latter: "Was not this ideal pitched too high at the outset? Yet monasticism like chivalry would not have been a motivating ideal for centuries had it not possessed a high worth, social, ethical, and aesthetic, for the development of society."[36] It must, however, be pointed out that the attitude of Erasmus was certainly not a novel one. The suppression of religious orders had been suggested in the great reform councils of the high Middle Ages. Nor did he go so far in his modified attack upon the institution as did Pope Paul III. As Bouyer points out, Erasmus' criticism of monasticism, as with other institutions of the Church, "bears always upon a fact, not on a principle."[37] Paul III's reform commission proposed the suppression of all existing orders by refusing them permission to accept postulants. It is interesting that the Vatican Council during the last century found not a few bishops and theologians who once again advocated the suppression of religious orders.

Since he believed the call to perfection was a summons to all Christians, Erasmus suggested that, instead of the monastic state being regarded as the only "religious" state, the entire world be looked on as a modified monastery: "quid aliud est civitas quam magnum monasterium?" Instead of the vows of poverty, chastity, and obedience, he urges that we keep and observe purely and with sincerity the first vow that we solemnly make to Christ when we receive Baptism. He sums up his whole Christocentric approach by exhorting: "But in every state of life let this be the common endeavor of all, that everyone according to his own ability endeavor to reach the goal [σμοπος] of Christ, which is open to all men, and that all of us encourage and help one another, neither envying those who overtake us

---

[36] J. Huizinga, *The Waning of the Middle Ages* (London, 1927), p. 94.

[37] Bouyer, *op. cit.*, p. 176.

in this course, nor disdaining those who out of weakness are unable to overtake us."[38]

For Erasmus, who knew too well from his own experience with the monks of St. Augustine at Steyn, that even the monks themselves fell short of this ideal, the absurdity of making second-class citizens out of all lay Christians was more than apparent. The crisis in monasticism in the early twelfth century pointed above all to the impossibility of imposing asceticism and its monastic framework on society as a whole. The failure of such misguided zeal not only broke up the equilibrium between monasticism and the world that had been the product of five centuries of interpenetration by Benedictine ideals of Western society, but marked the beginning of the separation between monastic and secular life that reached an unhappy climax in the late Middle Ages. The mendicants of the following centuries, forming as they did a sort of *corps élite* under the direction of the papacy also failed to impose the ideals of the Gospel on Western society. The prophetic and evangelical vocation of the friars became subordinated to the demands of ecclesiastical power politics thus producing a rift in the reform movement from which medieval Christendom never recovered. The disproportionally large number of defections from among the monastic group during the sixteenth century, both in the older orders as well as in the mendicants, bears out this point.

In a certain sense Erasmus advocated substituting for "the contemplative asceticism of the monks" the "asceticism of disciplined work." He sums up his beliefs in this regard in his lengthy letter to the Benedictine Abbot Wolz:

> But I desire with all my heart, and have no doubt that all who are sincerely religious-minded also desire, that the religion of the Scriptures be so pleasant to every man that being content with it, they do not seek the religion of Benedictines or Franciscans. . . . I would that all Christian men should so live that those whom we call religious would appear less religious, which of course today is quite evident, for why should I try

---

[38] Allen, *op. cit.*, III, 377.

to conceal what is so manifestly evident. . . . In ancient times, as I have said, the religious life was nothing other than a life of seclusion. Today we use the term to refer to those who are completely drowned in the affairs of the world and who exercise a certain tyranny in human matters. And yet because of their particular cult, their title, or I know not what, they have attributed to themselves such sanctimoniousness that they no longer recognize anyone else as Christians. Why do we make so straight and narrow the religion of Christ when He would make it so wide?[39]

He continually stresses the asceticism of the person living in the world:

What would be more wicked than to give to you the same reward as others while letting a certain few bear the labors on which the reward is based. What would be more wanton than to wish to rule jointly with the Head, while not wishing to suffer with Him? Therefore, do not look at what others do and flatter yourself by comparison with them. To die to sin is indeed a hard thing and one known to a very few monks. And yet this is the common profession of all Christians. Once in Baptism you swore fealty to this. What can be more sacred or religious than this vow? Either we must perish, or without exception, by this way proceed to salvation. He who decides to become a Christian has already chosen the better part of Christianity.

He points out in the Third Rule of the *Enchiridion* that the only true way to virtue is the way of Christ and that life itself is a form of asceticism: "What kind of life can you find free from sadness and hardships? . . . In marriage how great is the weight of family care — misery that they who are not experiencing it fail to see? How much danger, toil and anxiety is there in public duties that have to be met? Wherever you look there is seen to be a tremendous amount of misfortune. The life of man is filled with tribulation which the righteous and wicked suffer in common. If you will find these difficulties in the way of Christ, they will serve to increase your merit."

The poverty of the religious order he would make the rule for all Christians. In an age when the repeated accusation

---

[39] *Ibid.*

against the Church was that it was too imbued with the spirit of greed, when few objects of religion were not associated with money, when the avarice of the monks was a byword, his admonition was needed. "You believe that only to monks was property forbidden and poverty imposed? You have erred, for it pertains to all Christians. The law punishes you if you take unto yourself what belongs to another. It does not punish you if you take your possessions away from a needy brother. Yet, even so, Christ will punish you."

Erasmus does not condemn monasticism so much as he points out that Christian perfection does not consist in a particular status, a special estate, an exclusive membership. J. P. Pineau, voicing a common misconception in this regard,[40] feels that Erasmus attacks the institution as such. What disturbs Erasmus is that too many monks rely on their being monks almost to the exclusion of their being Christians. In other writings he points out that there is always a danger in assuming that this or that vocation is perfection independently of Christ. Thus he points out that piety does not consist in celibacy or virginity if these do not point to Christ.[41] If the Church in the late Middle Ages had become overinstitutionalized, then so had many of the religious orders within its framework. In fact, the centripetal forces so resented by transalpine Catholics at the time were implemented for the most part by the mendicants with their episcopal immunities.

It is a well-known fact, and remains in evidence today, that the papacy is only too wont to bring independent lay movements under its direction and control by giving them a monastic garb. The early Franciscan movement, for example, was not intended by its founder to be an organized religious institution. The *Devotio Moderna* achieved its finest results as long as it remained a lay movement more or less independent of ecclesiastical direction. There are few instances in which Erasmus does not direct

---

[40] J. Pineau, *Erasme, Sa pensée religieuse* (Paris, 1924), p. 126.

[41] "Neque enim coelibatus aut virginitas, per se virtus est, si non spectet ad Christum." *Erasmi Opera Omnia,* IX, 974.

his criticism against an exaggerated image of status piety. Yet in this respect it is necessary to bear in mind that he is not at all at variance with the traditional teaching of the Church on this subject. Thomas Aquinas is at pains to point out that the monastic life is not a state of perfection but rather a means to perfection. Nor does he at all imply that it is the sole means. Erasmus follows Thomas in his insistence that the perfection of the Christian life consists essentially in charity and only secondarily in the observance of the counsels. ("Per se quidem et essentialiter consistit perfectio christianae vitae in charitate. . . . Secundario autem et instrumentaliter perfectio consistit in counsiliis."[42])

Erasmus is often misunderstood in his criticism of monasticism. He is not opposed to it as an institution. In fact he often praises the monastic state and speaks of the monk as the "pure christianus." The monastery is nothing other than a flock harmonizing in the purest doctrine of Christ.[43] What he does oppose, however, is the monopolizing of the notion "religious" by those dedicated to the monastic life. The monks call themselves religious although many of them have nothing to do with religion. To identify the word "religious" with a particular status or a particular calling is for him tantamount to blasphemy. (The term is used indiscriminately even to this day — how often we hear the expression, so-and-so has entered "religion.") Every Christian has been chosen from out of this world and dedicated to God in a very special way. Erasmus' objection to a limitation of the word "religious" is based upon the same argument that he raises against the assumption that the Church is identified with the priesthood alone or that the laity are, in contrast, to be equated with the "worldly." It is his belief that all Christians are religious.[44] With Jerome he asserts that whoever does not desire to be perfect has really no desire to be good. The obligation

---

[42] *Summa Theologica,* II-II, 184, 3.

[43] "Nec aliud monasterium, quam grex ultro conspirans in purissimam Christi doctrinam." *Ibid.,* V. 1054.

[44] "Abitror omnes Christianos esse religiosos." *Ibid.,* IX, 637.

to perfection flows from membership in the Christian community. It is in this sense that Erasmus looks upon the world as a vast monastery. And there is no reason why membership should be limited to a few: "Cur professionem omnium communem ad paucos contrahimus?"[45] The vow we make at Baptism contains an obligation to strive after perfection that constitutes an absolute and continuous demand.

For Erasmus every Christian attains perfection insofar as he follows his particular calling as a partner with his Creator. Like St. Anthony of Florence before him and like St. Francis de Sales after him, Erasmus saw the inconsistency of trying to transplant the spiritual norms of the cloister into the world. The perfectibility of an individual must of necessity be conditioned to the situation in which he finds himself. The "collatio omnium ad Christum, unicum scopus," the referring of all to Christ, the single objective, the one goal, is the basic formula for perfection; it is a formula that transcends situations, a norm that can be utilized with the best results and with the greatest immediacy of all, regardless of its user's situation in life. This Christocentric approach avoids the danger that is often hidden in the performance of religious acts or the acceptance of religious dogmas: the danger of unconsciously failing to associate the act or dogma with Christ. This is the danger of increasing the distance between the individual and the Logos, of forming, as it were, a barrier zone that threatens to destroy the living contact between Christ and the individual. The great danger in all religious experience — egocentrism — is eliminated in this approach, which is wonderfully expressed in the Liturgy: "in Him, and with Him, and through Him."

The threat envisioned by Erasmus in all of his theological works was that of the invisible Church being absorbed into the visible. His convictions on this point flowed from his spirituality. "When the corporal presence of Christ is useless to salvation should we then dare to establish perfect piety in any corporal

---

[45] *Ibid.*, V, 854.

thing?" "To worship Christ in things visible, for the sake of things visible, and in these to place the highest part of religion . . . and by these visible things to be called away from Christ, when they are really intended to lead to Him — this is certainly to revolt from the law of the Gospel which is spiritual." How reminiscent this last remark is of the words of the late Cardinal Archbishop of Paris: "to stop at the juridical organization and go no further than external appearances is to replace the Body of Christ by a corpse of the Church."[46]

Thus the great efforts by Erasmus to elucidate the peace of Christ, the basic principle by which the visible Church can be identified as the authentic expression of the invisible. He introduces the *Enchiridion* by pointing out that there is no other condition of peace than to fight with all our might against vice.

Erasmus' concern for peace is usually treated as the expression of a sensitive and retiring scholarly temperament, or as his seemingly innate political conservatism. But there are adumbrations of a concern for the reign of Christ's interior peace in each soul. In the *Enchiridion* interior peace seems to be largely a matter of a quiet conscience. He writes that no pleasure is lacking where there is not lacking the pleasure of a quiet conscience. In his work on *Ecclesiastical Concord* he recommends "that peace, which according to the blessed Paul 'surpasses all understanding,' and which alone keeps and protects our minds and bodies from all evils in the Pacificator Jesus Christ Our Lord."[47] For Erasmus, peace among the brethren of Christ, which he identifies with mutual charity, is the fundamental commandment of the Gospel. This thought recurs again and again in the *Querella Pacis*. "What other things do His commandments, His parables, inculcate and repeat, but peace, but mutual charity? Departing this world, He commanded peace, which He had so commanded throughout His life. 'Love one another,' He said, 'as I have loved you.' And again, 'I give

---

[46] E. Suhard, *Growth or Decline* (Chicago, 1948), p. 28.
[47] *Erasmi Opera Omnia*, V, 469.

you My peace, I leave you My peace.' The Eucharist is the convenant of peace. What does the communion of that holy bread and amiable cup decree but a certain new and indissoluble concord?"[48]

Thus peace is a condition for the acceptability of divine worship, and in this Erasmus does nothing but repeat the Gospel injunction that a man must go and be reconciled with his brother before offering sacrifice to God. It can then be understood why, on the most solid of theological grounds, peace is absolutely essential to the Church of Christ and why Erasmus can say with St. Ambrose, "Pax . . . est nostra religio."

Those who ascribe Erasmus' irenicism to his scholarly quietude and conservative temperament are not entirely wrong, yet it is quite obvious that peace in the visible Church, and in society generally, is, for him, the expression of the innermost law of the invisible Church. Peace is, further, a necessary condition for all good things. In the *Querella Pacis*, Peace eulogizes herself in contrast with war: "I, Peace, be the fountain, parent, nourisher, augmenter, and defender of all good things, that either the air or the earth hath; . . . without me nothing flourishes nowhere, nothing sure, nothing pure or holy. . . ."[49]

The unanimity that is so essential to Christian peace is to be achieved not by force but by persuasion. Here Erasmus brings in his idea of Christian liberty, which he describes as the free and eager submission to God's law, rather than the mere absence of external restraint. He sums this up in the *Enchiridion,* when he remarks that no one is more obedient to his Head than he who, inspired with the Holy Spirit, is free in that liberty. In the Cleve Church Ordinances which he inspired, his thoughts are similarly expressed: "Those who love God and hear His word shall comply with it and not consider Christian freedom as external only or the freedom of the flesh, but will generously do that which is required by law and out

---

[48] *Querella Pacis,* ed. W. Hirten (New York, 1946), pp. 18-21.
[49] *Ibid.,* pp. 7-8.

of charity will be willing and ready to serve others." The very foundation of liberty is charity itself. "True piety, which flourishes only when the spirit spontaneously strives to grow in charity, withers when the spirit sluggishly reposes in external ceremonies, chosen for it by others."[50] There can be no doubt that Erasmus tends to neglect the notion of the Church as an external institution, yet the neglect stems not so much from a dissatisfaction with certain aspects of the exterior structure as it does from an insistence on its interior and invisible aspects. The Church is above all a living community whose unity is destroyed only by him who would tamper with its inner bond of charity; it is the self-evident arena of all religious life. In short he wishes to make religion a more dynamic part of everyday life, and often finds the superstructure of the Church in the way of this attempt. He does not advocate a destruction of the juridical framework, but rather a shifting of emphasis.

The *Enchiridion* begins with the impressive preface, "we must be watchful in life." Erasmus had no illusions about the strength of human nature. Neither the self-sufficiency of the Italian humanists whom he knew so well nor the complacency of his contemporaries could delude him here. He knows human weakness too well, and makes a point at the very outset of his treatise of warning his readers of self-delusion. Yet at the same time he is vitally aware that the power of evil in the world has been broken once and for all by the triumph of Christ and that this triumph must be effected in individual lives — the obligation of completing this victory is incumbent upon all. Once he has indicated the perils that threaten the spiritual safety of the Christian, he indicates the means that are to be used in triumphing over the omnipresent snares of the Evil One. He speaks of the arms of the militant Christian. The Christian is no longer the medieval pilgrim with cord and staff; he is the soldier armed with the sword of the spirit. The period of incubation is over.

---

[50] J. P. Dolan, *The Erasmian Influence in the Cleve Church Ordinances* (Münster, 1958), p. 10.

The first of the arms he recommends is prayer, a prayer that is not, he exhorts, a mere external, mechanical thing but an exercise that bears on the projection of Christ into everyday life. As a second weapon he advocates the reading and study of those writers of antiquity whose thoughts have been so influential in the formation of the Western mind. Since its very beginning Christianity has posed the question: Does secular learning contribute to spiritual growth or hinder it? The problem never, of course, assumed the magnitude that it now has, when scientific knowledge divorced from moral values has reached a point where man's growing mastery of the physical world carries with it the threat of racial suicide. Yet the basic problem in the relation of learning to the spiritual life is posed by Erasmus' belief that among the ancients a formative influence could be found for the new world he hoped to see born.

In the first chapter of the *Enchiridion* he establishes the basis of his doctrine on piety. It is in certain respects an Augustinian approach: the restlessness of man in this world. Based on the conviction that God has created us for Himself and we are restless until we rest in Him, this approach considers religion as basically a personal relationship between God and man. The frequently rather cheap playing off of "life" against "doctrine," or ethics against theology, is not in keeping with the situation envisioned by Erasmus, who saw that in early Christianity these aspects were inseparably connected. It was plain to him, as to St. Paul, that Christianity was neither a philosophical system nor a particular set of morals, neither an intellectual movement nor a code of ethics; rather it was participation in life — in divine life.

In presenting the life of the Christian as a "type of perpetual warfare" and in speaking of the "weapons" needed in the conflict, Erasmus is applying a metaphor that is as old as Christianity itself. St. Paul uses it frequently: "Let us put on the armor of light"; "we do not make war according to the flesh; for the weapons of our warfare are not carnal." And St. Jerome often speaks similarly in his writings. The appropriateness of the metaphor cannot go unnoticed in the mobilized world of today.

The idea of the dignity of man, which is so prominent in the entire Handbook is, of course, an ancient one. Man as a microcosm, distinguished by speech and reason from the rest of the created world, is the repeated theme of ancient literature. The early Christian emphasis on the salvation of mankind and upon the incarnation of Christ carried with it the idea of a special position of man in the world. This idea was taken by the Fathers and fused with the notions inherited from pagan antiquity. Like the Italian humanists, especially Pico and Ficino, Erasmus was interested not so much in philosophical speculation as in the development of a cultural and educational ideal based on the study and imitation of classical literature. In the *Enchiridion* the classics are recommended for the Christian layman not only because they train his mind in the art of appreciating the good, the true, and the beautiful, but above all because they have so much in them conducive to righteous living ("ad recte vivendum conducibilia").

The classics are the preparatory school for a deeper appreciation of the dignity of man. The Christian learns more from the classics than the sanctity of knowledge; he learns self-understanding. This idea is perhaps best expressed by Augustine, when he says, "Noverim me Domine, noverim Te — I must know myself in order to know Thee, O Lord." The writings of the ancients cannot be overstressed in preparing an individual to know himself. Not only do they instill a fine sense of morality, but they lead to an awareness of one's self as a human being, which is essential for living a Christian life. The classics are also needed for an appreciation of the Scriptures. The mediocrity of Catholic biblical scholarship today is due, in no small part, to neglect of the classics (despite a pretense of studying them) in preparatory schools.

One way in which knowledge of the classics aids Scripture study, in Erasmus' view, is by making us wary of interpreting Holy Writ only in a literal sense. The allegorical nature of the writing, so long as it is recognized as such, is of great aid in arriving at the deeper sense of Scripture. This concern is rooted in the desire to see in the Scriptures a living God, rather than a mere conceptual abstraction of the divine, to see the lesson in the miracle as well as the divine power. It is here again that the position of Erasmus exhibits a certain timelessness. His insistence on the allegorical sense of Scripture runs contrary to the trend, so popular today, of stripping away the mythology of the Scriptures (the *entmythologisierung* of Bultman) and seeking the alleged "kernel" of the Christian message. The mythological element for Erasmus is essential to understanding the true nature of Christ as the Logos. The classics afford the balance that will avoid an overemphasis on either literal or allegorical interpretation.

Finally, the classics — especially the poetry of the ancients — are recommended because "these sciences fashion and quicken a child's mind" and form as it were the ABC's of wisdom. They are a means to an end and they are justified as a prelude to the highest study of which man's mind is capable, the study of the Scriptures. They are profitable above all "if everything be applied and referred to Christ" *(si omnia ad Christum referantur)*. One is reminded of Newman's view on education: "the literature of Greece, continued into, and enriched by the literature of Rome, together with the studies which it involves has been the instrument of education, and the food of civilization, from the first times of the world down to this day . . . it may even be called the soil out of which Christianity grew."[51] Newman answers the question of how best to strengthen, refine, and enrich the intellectual powers in an almost identical way with Erasmus: "The perusal of the poets, historians and philosophers of Greece will accomplish this."[52] And like Erasmus, he sees that "the grace stored in Jerusalem and the gifts which radiate from Athens, are made over and concentrated in Rome. To

---

[51] J. Newman, *The Idea of a University* (New York, 1960), p. 199.
[52] *Ibid.,* p. 200.

separate these distinct teachings, human and divine, that meet in Rome is to retrograde."[53]

In emphasizing the role of the classics in preparing the Christian for life in the world, Erasmus is merely following the example of the Fathers of the Church — Jerome, Augustine, Basil, Cyprian — who are in accord in giving the ancient writers a place in the Christian scheme of learning.

Perhaps the finest appraisal of the kind of approach to the study of divine things favored by Erasmus is found in a letter addressed by St. Thomas More in 1518 to the University of Oxford, where a number of scholastics had ridiculed the classics. Answering the objections raised by a particular person, More says:

> Now as to the question of humanistic education being secular. No one has ever claimed that a man needed Greek and Latin, or indeed any education, in order to be saved. Still, this education which he calls secular does train the soul in virtue. In any event few will question that humanistic education is the chief, almost the sole reason why men come to Oxford. Children can receive a good education at home from their mother; all except cultivation and book reading. Besides, not every one that comes to you does so immediately to pursue theological studies. It is proper that some should also pursue law, in which case the wisdom that comes from the study of humane things is requisite. And in any case it is something not useless to theologians; without such study they might possibly preach a sermon acceptable to an academic group but they would certainly fail to reach the common man. Now from whom could they acquire such skill in a better manner than from the classical poets, orators, and historians?
> Moreover, there are some who through a knowledge of things natural construct a ladder by which to rise to the contemplation of things supernatural; they build a path to theology through philosophy and the liberal arts, which this man condemns as secular; they adorn the Queen of Heaven with the spoils of Egypt. This fellow declares that only theology should be studied, but if he admits even that, I don't see how he can accomplish his aim without some knowledge of languages, whether Hebrew, or Greek, or Latin, unless of course the elegant gentleman has convinced himself that there is enough theology in English or that all theology can be squeezed into

---

[53] *Ibid.,* p. 201.

the limit of those scholastic "quaestiones" which are posed and answered, and for which, I must admit, a modicum of Latin suffices.

But, really, I cannot admit that theology, that august Queen of Heaven, can thus be confined. Does she not dwell and abide in the Holy Scriptures? Does she not pursue her pilgrim way through the cells of the holy Fathers, Augustine, and Jerome, Ambrose and Cyprian, Chrysostom, Gregory, Basil and their like? The study of theology was solidly based on these now desposed expositors of fundamental truth during all the Christian centuries until the invention of these petty and meretricious "quaestiones" which alone today are tossed so glibly back and forth.

Further: this fellow, just to show how immoderate he could be in a sermon, specifically called students of Greek, "heretics," teachers of Greek, "chief devils," and pupils of Greek, "lesser devils"; and the zeal of this holy man drove him to call by the name of devil one whom everyone knows the devil himself could hardly bear to see occupy a pulpit. He did everything but name that one [Erasmus], as everybody realized just as clearly as they realized the folly of the speaker.[54]

It is interesting that the study of the classics urged by Erasmus and More was reiterated in the seminary legislation of the Council of Trent, largely through the influence of the English cardinal, Reginald Pole. Erasmus' critical work on the New Testament was of vital importance in the proceedings of this great Council.

Once Erasmus establishes that learning is an essential element of true piety, he uses it as the only true approach to the Scriptures. One must study the Scriptures with a mind sharpened by the culture of the ancients and a heart purified by reverence, thereby penetrating beneath their surface and understanding the inner meaning of their words. Here again we see how Erasmus was, in a sense, centuries ahead of his time. The growing trend today to emphasize the kerygmatic nature of the Gospels, with the aim of vivifying the force of Christian teaching, is what he actually recommends. Today this aim expresses itself in the attempt to convey the greatness of Christ not by means of an

---

[54] E. Rogers, *The Correspondence of Sir Thomas More* (Princeton, 1947), p. 11ff.

abstract list of divine attributes but by concrete examples. We have made the rediscovery that true paradise is to be found in man himself; heaven has come into his soul. The material paradise was but a symbol and the consequence of the richness of his soul.

Following Erasmus, we must see the Old Testament as our pedagogue in Christ and we must understand it from a Christological point of view. We must, with St. Paul, point to the central mystery of our religion, the very center of Apostolic teaching, "the mystery which had been hidden from ages and generations, which is Christ." In Christ are contained in germ, and revealed, all the mysteries of Christianity, even that of the Blessed Trinity. Christ alone is able to lead us to the Father, to introduce us — by different ways — into the sanctuary of the Trinity: now by His divine-human dignity, now by His theandric work. Because Christ is truly God, He surpasses our most daring hopes. Because He is man, blood of our blood, we believe in His understanding of our weakness and miseries. He is the mediator between God and man, His own person throwing a bridge across the bottomless abyss separating Divinity from humanity.

In explaining his idea of the relation of piety to Holy Scripture, Erasmus places an importance on the allegorical method of interpretation that has been for the most part neglected by his critics. In his *Ratio Verae Theologiae* he points out that, after the manner of St. Paul, Jewish ceremonies must be allegorized for Christians and that the scriptural commentator will find in both the New and the Old Testament certain passages whose historical sense is otherwise absurd or contrary to the majesty of God, as when God is said to have been angry, or when Christ is said to have been led to a high mountain to survey the kingdoms of the earth.

We see here a certain predilection for Origen, whom Erasmus calls the greatest of the commentators. Origen's spiritual teaching held that Christians progressed through three stages of piety — physical, psychical, and spiritual — by moving from the literal to the moral and thence to the mystical sense of

Scripture. Thus true piety, piety of the spirit, is not nourished by knowledge of Scripture pure and simple, for without the spiritual sense, some parts of Scripture are of less value for piety than the works of the pagan poets.

Thus the first section of the *Enchiridion* lays the basis for Erasmus' teaching on the doctrine of piety. He points out that by nature man is composed of both spiritual and corporeal elements and goes to great length to prove this from the writings of Scripture, tradition, and philosophy. Once he has established this duality, he lays down certain general norms or regulations that will be conducive to piety. The Fourth Rule is concerned with the Christocentric aspect of the spiritual life. Here he asks that "you set before you Christ as the only goal of your whole life, to whom alone you dedicate all zeal, all effort, all leisure and business." This is Erasmus' constant effort: to break through the narrow confinement and isolation that keep religion out of the arena of public life. For him "bene agere" is nothing other than to consider all in Christ ("in Christum spectare"). And yet the Christ who is to be the object and model of all our earthly strivings is not merely Christ the Divine teacher, or Christ the Divine exemplar, He is, above all, Christ the Divine Redeemer.

Those who would relegate Erasmus to the position of a mere rationalist moralist overlook his insistence on the role of Christ as our Redeemer. Through Christ, he says, we are reborn, we are re-established in our pristine integrity ("Quod autem aliud est Christi philosophia, quam ipse renascentiam vocat, quam instauratio bene conditae naturae"). His emphasis on Christ as our exemplary cause revolves about and is based upon the role of Christ as our redemptive savior.

The Fifth Rule lays down the basic rule for Christian living: through the visible things of the world to the invisible ("per visibilia ad invisibilia"). An impassioned plea for a return to the realization of the inwardness of the spiritual life reaches its peak in this rule. In a world not unlike our own, where religion had largely become a matter of ceremonies and conventional observances, Erasmus endeavors to restate the essential character of religion, the cult of the invisible. The Apostles themselves, privileged as they were with the physical presence of Christ, remained weak and childish until the bodily presence was replaced by the Spirit in their hearts. The Sixth Rule brings out the image of Christ as the prototype of genuine piety in every station of life. In the concluding section Erasmus lists remedies against particular vices and, although there is little original in the presentation, he nonetheless adds a concrete dimension to these remedies by situating them in the stream of daily events. The author makes the whole purpose of the little book clear from the outset; it is aimed not at making the reader learned but rather at making him pious. He will not preach retirement from the world, but holiness in the world. He wants to present to the layman a simple, direct, and objective compendium of what it means to live a Christian life in the world.

In his letter to the Philippians, St. Paul writes: "But I press on hoping that I may lay hold of that for which Christ Jesus has laid hold of me. Brethren, I do not consider that I have laid hold of it already. But one thing I do . . . I press on towards the goal."[55] Following Jerome and Gregory of Nazianzus, Erasmus takes the Greek σκόπος, or "target," as the basis for his Christocentric theology.

"Nothing if not Christ or because of Christ" ("nihil nisi Christum aut propter Christum") is the whole tenor of the Christian life. All must center in or about Christ. Christ is the measure of all things because he is the source and the goal of all. Only when things live in Christ do they fulfill their worth. All things must be referred to Christ ("omnia ad Christum referantur"). In contrast to Thomas a Kempis, Erasmus does not take an either-or attitude toward the created world; he endeavors rather to see in the visible world around us the raw material which we must orientate toward Christ. The Christo-

---

[55] Phil. 3:13-14.

centrism of the *Devotio Moderna,* typified in the *Imitation of Christ,* is too exclusive. For Erasmus, everything — learning, health, wealth, physical beauty — are from Christ and must serve to project Christ into the world.

We cannot agree with the eminent German historian, Joseph Lortz, who holds that the damage Erasmus wrought in the Church far outweighs the good he did. Nothing could be more false than Lortz's allegation that Erasmus and his teachings manifest the fundamental weaknesses of humanism: relativism, superficiality, and divorce of life from doctrine. Erasmus is wrong because he did not attain the heroic, we are told. How many Christians ever do? Lortz writes: "Untrustworthy and unstable, he would never venture to risk fame or life by whole-hearted entry into the lists for his principles or his friends. He is distinguished by indefiniteness, vacillation, indecision and far-reaching compromise. He does not possess the forceful definiteness that must be associated with dogma. He is a soulful relativist guided by sentiment. Christianity becomes moralism."[56] For Lortz, Erasmus is a precursor of Luther. His criticism of the Church is entirely subversive and threatens the unity of the Church with disruption when applied to the role of Scriptural interpretation. Nowhere does he take into consideration the absolute.

If Erasmus continually stresses that his Christian view of life is more a concern of the heart than of the understanding, more life itself than learning, he also sets his theology within the framework of religious behavior. For him, the only effective theology is one accompanied by piety. Theology and piety are intrinsically bound up with one another. His preference for the theological writers of antiquity is based to a certain extent upon the fact that he considers them pious individuals; they reflect "pia doctrina" and "docta pietas." A true theologian lives the things that he reads and preaches. It is not enough to comprehend the Scriptures with understanding; they must penetrate

---

[56] J. Lortz, *History of the Church* (Milwaukee, 1938), pp. 329-30.

the heart as well, for a theologian who does not understand himself cannot understand other truths. If a simpler and more pious theology is the ideal, then it must find its source in the Scriptures and the writings of the Fathers. This is how Erasmus sums up his purpose in this field: "I have endeavored to recall theology, which has fallen into sophisticated squabbling, back to its source and original simplicity" ("Theologiam minium ad sophisticas argutias delapsam, ad fontes ac priscam simplicitatem revocare conatus sum").

The accusation that Erasmus reduces theology to mere moral exhortation, or a religion of the Moral Rearmament type, is unfounded. If Erasmus disagreed with the schoolmen, it was not because of their fundamental doctrine, it was because of the methods they used to convey the truth and for the "barbarism" of their expressions. In his view, if their doctrines did not lead to better Christian behavior, then there was something radically wrong with them. He avoided going into the background of his simplified Christianity. The busy Christian of his day had not the leisure for this. It might surprise contemporary critics of Erasmus to read his defense and praise of Thomas Aquinas, particularly for the latter's acquaintance with the literature of antiquity, a defense that Erasmus offered to his friend, John Colet.[57] P. Mesnard says of the theology of Erasmus:

> The theology of Erasmus rests in fact on the central idea of divine perfection. An all-powerful God, of infinite goodness, has shown forth His power and His goodness in the order of creation. His creatures owe Him everything: it is thus an insult to their creator to cast a doubt on the consubsistent reality of the natural order. But out of His excessive goodness and in spite of the rejection of His first advances, God endows man with the possibility of obtaining the exceptional privilege of final blessedness; to reach it, the fallen nature of man is doubly in need of being infused with supernatural life. This is the work of grace which restores nature and carries it beyond itself by enlightening and strengthening free will.[58]

In essence this is the doctrine of Thomas: man cannot merit

---

[57] F. Seebohm, *The Oxford Reformers* (London, 1869), p. 105.
[58] P. Mesnard, *Essai sur le Libre Arbitre* (Paris, 1959), p. 60.

grace in the first place, or achieve by himself final perfection, but he may earn, by striving, an increase of the grace already received.

It certainly cannot be said that Erasmus was ignorant of the teachings of the Scholastics. His studies at the University of Paris and at the University of Louvain, the two fountain-heads of scholastic learning in the Europe of his day, had given him more than a sufficient knowledge of their doctrines. He did far more than note their bad Latin and the vapidness of their arguments. The fact that he received a doctorate in theology is sufficient evidence that he had mastered what was then an essential requirement for such a degree. If he disliked the Schoolmen, it was not for their fundamental doctrines as much as for the methods they used. He found too much in their systems that provided the foundations for the mechanistic view of religion that he fought throughout his entire life. The memorizing of arguments and the doling out of capsulary mottoes were not, for him, adequate substitutes for a return to the spiritual ideals of the Scriptures.

Perhaps the most urgent reason for his rejection of the Scholastics was that their endless hairsplitting was making the message of Christ less and less intelligible for the common man. In defending his *Enchiridion,* many years after it was published, he wrote to the Benedictine Abbot Paul Volz:

> Therefore I am not bothered by the mockery of certain individuals who despise this little book as being neither erudite nor clerical, insisting that it might just as well have been a primer for a child learning the alphabet since it makes no references to the questions of Scotus. It is not intended to prepare them for disputations in the schools; rather may it at least make them inclined to keep the peace of Christ. It is not intended to prepare for disputation in theology but rather for leading a divine life. Today there are almost as many commentaries on the Master of Sentences as there are clerics. There is neither measure nor number of the Summas which, like apothecaries, mix various elements together, making out of what is used a new prescription and out of what is fresh something stale, out of compounds a single product, and out of a single element many compounds. How could these volumes

help us to live in a Christian manner, when no one could even
leaf through them in the period of a lifetime?[59]

In evaluating the theology of Erasmus we must bear in
mind that this great humanist had no more intention of develop-
ing a speculative system of theology or philosophy than he had
of leading a third party in the religious disputes of the sixteenth
century. The century-old squabble between Thomists and Scot-
ists and between advocates of the *via antiqua* and the *via
moderna* were in his mind the real cause of the neglect of
Christian piety in his day. Taking up a definite theological
position was a move that he made only reluctantly when he
was forced to by attack or pressure from above. Pope Adrian,
in his appeal to Erasmus to take up the cudgels against Luther,
invited him to Rome where he would have the advantage of
liberty and the society of learned theologians. The offer of a
Cardinal's hat was the one thing Erasmus scorned, and there is
no doubt that he shared the sentiments of Dante, who wrote
three centuries before that there were no theologians in Rome.[60]
Yet it is significant that the only truly reform-minded pope of
the times, who so frankly acknowledged the culpability of the
Roman curia for the troubles assailing Christendom, saw in
Erasmus a hope for healing the abuses in the Church. There
is little doubt that Paul III would have bestowed the Cardinal's
hat upon Erasmus had he lived.

The study of the philosophy of Christ should lead to piety,
not to disputations, Erasmus states in the introduction to the
*Enchiridion*. Not only is a preoccupation with subtle and in-
soluble problems fruitless, but it leads to discord and strife.
The goal of theology was to be found in life itself rather than
in disputation ("vita magis quam disputatio"); in transformation rather than a "rationale" ("transformatio magis quam
ratio"). Erasmus' deep knowledge of the Fathers awakened
him to the all-important fact that the conceptual approach to

---

[59] Allen, *op. cit.*, III, 363.
[60] Dante, *Paradiso*, Canto IX.

religion was not enough. Also needed was the *theologia practica* that Gerson had preached a century before at the University of Paris. For a century the cry for reform in theology had gone unheard. With the Church for the most part secularized and with the logical-metaphysical occupation of the clergy becoming a scandal almost as disastrous as the immoral example of their lives, it was no wonder that Gerson urged the preachers of his day to limit themselves to explaining to the people the basic truths of Christianity: the Ten Commandments, the theological virtues, and the articles of the Creed.

In the eyes of this Chancellor of the University of Paris the process of multiplying ecclesiastical statutes had completely removed from the minds of the faithful the ideal of Christ, the Christ whose yoke was light and whose commandments were aimed at making salvation less burdensome. Gerson pointed out time and time again that the clergy thought they could rule the Church better with man-made laws than with the law of the Gospel. The accumulation of unimportant legislation, equated as it was with the divine law, had the dire result of reducing the divine law itself to ridicule. Like Erasmus, Gerson asks: "What would Augustine think, what would be his sorrow, if he were to visit these times and see the incredible variety and the dissonant multiplicity of burdensome man-made laws so extensive that they are incapable of enumeration and through which as through a series of traps and nets one can hardly expect to pass without being trapped."[61] As with Erasmus, the main brunt of Gerson's attack was borne by the religious orders, most of which endeavored to capitalize on the disturbances within the Church and the state at the time. The sermons delivered by the members of these orders were taken from the

---

[61] O sapiens Augustinus, quid nostra tempestate dixisses; ubi pro varietate et motu capitam incredibilis est varietas et dissona multiplicitatis onerum huismodi servilium et humanarum prout loqueris praesumptionum; inter quas velut inter laqueos animarum et ligantia retia vix quispiam securus et indeprensus incesserit. Gerson, *Opera De Vit. Sp.*, ed. Dupin (Antwerp, 1706), III, 16.

unintelligible texts of the Scholastics or the memorized sermons of other preachers.

Gerson and Erasmus shared a disdain for the juridic theology that had been so much a part of medieval Christianity (nurtured by the necessitarian philosophy of Aristotle). The monkish ideal with its flight from the world might have been an answer for an earlier period when Roman society was disintegrating, but the emergence of a bourgeois society brought in its wake the conviction that the city of man was not necessarily the work of Satan. The awareness of the struggle between the enfeoffed mentality of the Middle Ages nurtured with the highly idealized aspirations of monasticism and the widening horizons of the bourgeois laity had been at work for over a century when Erasmus appeared on the scene. Christianity had to be adapted to the changing times. The new world of the merchant, banker, and financier was making the causistry of the cenobite uncomfortably out of place. The theme that Innocent III had imposed upon his world — that man was formed out of dust and born to labor, sorrow, and fear — was losing its hold on the fifteenth-century mind. Individualism was breaking up the medieval universalism. The fifteenth-century problem of the proper relationship between the individual and society was one of which Gerson was extremely aware. The *vita contemplativa* and the *vita activa* could no longer be defined in the old religious terms.

The century that separated Gerson from Erasmus had witnessed an unabated multiplication of those very evils in theology that the great theologian of Paris had striven to counteract. The great schism had been healed, only to give way to a secularized papacy. The papal states were hardly distinguishable from the emerging Renaissance bodies that Machiavelli was to extol in his writings. Yet the restitution of either the theocratic Empire or the theocratic Church was irreconcilable with the new age. The case for and against the papacy had long become stereotyped; the accumulation of these pros and cons was so vast that it is amazing that a true vision of either secular or ecclesiastical government could have survived in the bloodless parchment combat. Reduction of everything to formulae had sapped the freshness of the medieval world. It was Gerson's lifelong endeavor to reconcile philosophy and theology, faith and knowledge, by putting them in a more practical sphere. His reform in theology was aimed at bringing it out of the fantastically unimaginative sterility into which it had fallen in order to direct it towards its primary purpose: increasing the love of God ("non in subtilis inquisitione veritatis sed in cultu charitatis consistit regnum dei").[62] Yet even his work, like the efforts of Nicholas of Cusa, was to come to naught because of an apathetic papacy beset, on the one hand, by an avaricious group of ecclesiastical politicians, and, on the other, by the ineptitude of an illiterate clerical proletariat. Erasmus, well aware of the failings of the leaders, directed his theology towards an intelligent laity whom he recognized as the leaders of the new age and through whom he hoped for the re-establishment of a new Christian order based upon the ideals and norms of Christ in the Gospel.

Erasmus was critical above all else of the fact that theology had become so polluted and overgrown with philosophical dialectic that it was no longer possible to discover Christ beneath this accumulation. Writing to the Archbishop of Canterbury, William Warham, in 1506, he laments the depraved notion of the Divine that is the result of the nonsense of the sophists.[63] Theology as it was taught by the overspeculative, hairsplitting Scholastics was entirely too complicated to be of any possible use for living a pious life. Who could possibly find his way through the labyrinth of the disputations they multiply? Who can find the Gospel behind the wall of quiddities and haecceities that the Scholastics throw up? It is necessary for a Christian philosophy to be presented in a way that everyone can understand and benefit from. His words grow bitter when he points out that for most theologians Aristotle means more than Christ.

---

[62] Gerson, *Opera*, IV, 389.
[63] Allen, *op. cit.*, I, 419.

The theologians of his time, with their complicated sophisms, their rationalistic formulae and their ever-increasing dogmatism, had made any real penetration of the faith of the Gospel impossible.

The aim of Erasmus' theology was to be an interiorization, a spiritualization of religious practice, a more personal affair between the individual soul and God. Erasmus was above all a practical man, and thus the importance he attaches to rhetoric and eloquence as bringing warmth and color and transmitting the living ideals of the Gospel. This practicality is the key to understanding his reform of theological teaching. To him the excessively rational and analytic theological method which was current before his time prevented the student and ultimately the Christian people from seeing theological realities as they actually are, i.e., in the living, breathing Christian. He wanted to restore unity to these realities by presenting them in the more concrete fashion of the scriptural writers and the Fathers.

It has often been stated that we live in an age of reappraisal, of reinterpretation. The assumption of historians that postulates the efficacy of ideas as the driving force of human progress is everywhere being seriously questioned. The Marxist notion that it is not the consciousness of men that determines their existence but their social existence that determines their consciousness is enjoying a widening acceptance. An uneasiness that has resulted from overexposure to an image culture has led many to mistrust reality. Ranke remarked that without the impulse of the present we would probably never desire to investigate what has taken place in the past. The crisis that faces the world today has been no small factor in reviving interest in one of the great minds of the past, for our crisis is not unlike that which Erasmus faced in the sixteenth century. His times saw a serious yearning for Christian unity, the threat of an anti-Christian alien force from the East, the need for adapting theology to the social and economic changes of the day, and these interests find their counterparts in the atomic age.

It is an amazing thing that an age which has paid such

adulation to the historian is so remiss in using knowledge in evaluating its own time. The dilemma facing Christianity today, the complexities involved in a pluralistic society, have been analyzed to the point of actually overlooking the temporal framework in which they operate. This preoccupation has, unfortunately, greatly weakened our sense of history at a time when it is more needed than ever before. In a technological age we must ever be cognizant that the facts which exist in the world are not only those of nature but also those which the historical process has produced. There must be an awareness of what we have gained, as well as what we have lost, in the course of time. There is an assumption on the part of many, for example, that those problems confronting the Church today that involve highly specialized knowledge and particular cultural sensibilities never existed in a previous age simply because of a lack of communication media. It is even more common to think that the tensions between liberal and conservative thought, between intellectual freedom and privileged coercion have not previously affected the Church. To make history merely an arsenal from which to draw anachronisms to hurl at would-be attackers is a folly that has often been repeated. Too often an attempt is made to work with theories that are not evolved from history and to interject them into history. More often this juxtaposition deals with theories that have been tried and found wanting. To present medieval scholasticism only in terms of its thirteenth century Aristotelian form or to depict the sixteenth century religious revolt as a rejection of the *magisterium* of the Church are examples of this mentality.

Yet in understanding the significance of Erasmus we must run the risk of comparing the world in which he lived with our own and seeing his importance in terms of the analogies and parallels that are found therein. His age was above all an age in which new values, new standards, and new aspirations were coming into open conflict with a world that was in many respects moribund. A new world was emerging that had time to look at itself in terms of comparison with another long since dead, yet still important because it had witnessed the central event of history. To depreciate the Catholic humanism that was so much an ingredient of Erasmus' age simply because it failed to achieve its aim, is to deny that the future can be developed out of the past or that tradition, whenever it has been weakened or obscured through usage or oblivion, cannot be once more made vital to man.

The spread of higher education during the past century has at least, in part, given birth to the *respublica literatorum* that was the dream of Erasmians. The tolerance that he advocated, his insistence that Christianity must necessarily find its fulfillment in the realm of thought, that it can be realized only in the arena of the educated mind, has its echo today. Certainly the hope he voiced "that the philosophy of Christ be accessible to everybody" is closer to realization than in his day. The disillusionment resulting from man's repeated failure to establish lasting peace has increased rather than diminished during recent years. Erasmus' "dulce bellum inexpertis" — war is sweet to those who have not experienced it — was never more appropriate than today. The conviction fostered by him that war was more a moral problem than a political expedient finds few who will not embrace it today.

There is a parallel too, in the present hope to reconcile the Communist world with the West, although there is little hope of this succeeding along Christian lines as long as theology limits itself to the narrow confines of particular methodologies and systematics or entangles itself more deeply in the web of rejuvenated formalism. The mutual immanence of the historical and the constructive elements is needed for this reconciliation. The remark of Erasmus concerning the hoped-for defeat of the Turkish menace of his day might well be applied to the situation that now exists between the Western world and the Marxist camp:

> Preparation is now being made for war against the Turks, and we ought to pray that regardless of the reason it has been undertaken, that it may not be to the benefit of a few but rather for the general and common profit of all mankind. But

what do you think would happen, if after they are defeated (and certainly they shall not all be killed in the conflict), we were to lay before them the works of Duns Scotus, Gabriel, Averroës or any such schoolmen, with the intention of persuading them to embrace Christianity. What will they think and imagine (for surely they are human beings) when they read all these thorny, cumbrous, inextricable, and subtle imaginings of formalities, quiddities and "relationes"? What will they do when they see the great doctors and teachers of religion and holiness disagreeing so vehemently among themselves?[64]

The same line of thought was expressed by Cardinal Seripando, later Papal Legate at the Council of Trent, when he contrasted the heretical movements in Germany with the storm that heretics loosed upon the Church after Constantine's day. "But how lamentable is the difference. Then the heretics were laid low by the theologians with their own weapons, the Scriptures; we thought to oppose them with Aristotle and now we have become the object of their scorn."[65]

The Leonine revival of Scholasticism, the overemphasis on what is often mistakenly called Thomism, has resulted in a flooding of the publishing world with a plethora of abstract religious tracts that hardly interest even the serious speculative reader. The necessitarian doctrine of Aristotle that reduces the omnipotent God of revelation to a metaphysical principle, which acts with inexorable necessity according to an eternally determined pattern, is a poor inspiration for Christian charity. The hylomorphic presentation of the sacraments has had a deadening effect. The hierocratic theology of the Middle Ages has given way to clerical *ipse dixitism*. The quantitative element in popular piety today, with its whirl of novenas and its stress on cumulative effects, deserves the warning of Erasmus to those who put too much stress on the externals of religion and thus ran the risk of self-deception.

There is a growing feeling, too, among the laity that the norms of Christian perfection inspired by those dedicated to

---

[64] *Ibid.*, III, 364.
[65] H. Jedin, *Papal Legate at the Council of Trent* (Herder, 1947), p. 112.

the life of the cloister are not adaptable to life in the twentieth century. It is a truism that most manuals of piety and the increasing number of books written for lay Christians are produced by men and women of religious orders who unconsciously color them with the ideals of monastic life. The unique phenomenon of generations of English-speaking Catholics receiving their religious indoctrination from men and women dedicated to the life of the evangelical counsels has a hidden danger that is causing many to question its propriety.

Erasmus attacks this double standard of Christian living which, growing out of an overemphasis on the institutional Church, assumes that salvation is more within the range of the clergy than the laity. For him, since there was one salvation, there was one way of approaching it. If separation from the world was necessary, this had to be reconciled with the fact that the world still continued to exist. The great need was for intensifying the inner element of religion, the life of the spirit. He wished to tone down the institutional devices, the techniques of automatic performance which aimed at stimulating the process of salvation and which were so much a part of organized monasticism. Many Catholics today delight in what they consider the childish simplicity of those dedicated to the religious life. The religious immaturity revealed by this unconscious dependence on such a source, is unfortunate. Too many Catholics suffer from this immaturity; thus their preoccupation with those externals of religion that Erasmus condemns with the proviso that "they are quite necessary for children in Christ, at least until they have become a little more mature."

Catechetical knowledge with a weekly sprinkling of Ligourian ethics is hardly adequate to cope with the problems of a materialistic world. Far too many find false security in mere membership in an organization. Attendance at Sunday Mass and the avoidance of sins against sex are too often the only criterion of the good Christian. For over four centuries the Church has been living in a state of siege, defending itself to a great extent behind the walls of Scholasticism and monasticism.

Belloc's assertion that Europe was the faith and the faith was
Europe confused conformity with universalism. The failure of
Christianity to take root in the underdeveloped areas in Asia and
Africa cannot be entirely ascribed to imperialism. The cramming
of our students with isolated doctrines, indigestible information,
dry-as-dust textbook theology coated with devotional frosting,
is no longer adequate. The "darts that assail us from every
side" are destroying the protective cocoon of such training more
than Churchmen care to admit. The growing antagonism between the educated Catholic layman on the one side and the
authoritarian cleric on the other is a dangerous one. To justify
fraud by pointing out that religion transcends the learning of
philosophers or the lessons of history, is merely to engender
suspicion. It was the *causa causarum* of the breakdown in
Christian unity in the time of Erasmus. A desire for a greater
participation in divine cult was one of the reasons that the
Reformers found such a popular backing.

The tendency today to emphasize the peripheral aspects of
religion to the exclusion of the essential, the practice of solving
moral problems in terms of canon law, and the substitution of
the superstructure, the scaffolding, for the inner core of Christianity, the Mystical Body, is the very danger envisioned by
Erasmus in his *Enchiridion*. Cardinal Suhard points out that
there is the danger of making the Body of the Church a corpse
by stressing the external, the juridical. His words on the crisis
in which the Church finds itself today have a familiar Erasmian
tone: "It will perhaps be the great honor of our time to have
started what others will carry through; a humanism in proportion to the world in God's plan. On this condition and
only this condition can the Church develop and become in
the near future what she was in the Middle Ages for the West,
the spiritual center of the world. The atheistic and anti-
Christian civilization which is spreading in our time, can give
way to a sacred culture, to a Christian transfiguration of life."[66]

---

[66] Suhard, *op. cit.*, p. 57.

Like Erasmus he stresses that it is in the realm of thought that this transfiguration must take place: "Need we add that this task is incumbent on the intellectuals. . . . The first apostolate at the present crossroads is in the realm of thought."[67] Like Erasmus he stresses the Christocentric element: "this spirituality will be pivoted on the Mystical Body . . . it will produce the triumph of Christ the King by realizing its Pleroma, the achievement of the total Christ."[68] Here in sum is the message of Erasmus, here is the program he develops in the *Enchiridion.* This is a vision of a more practical Christianity founded on an ethical code that centers about a Divine Person, a Person in whom and through whom all finds meaning.

We have the account of Erasmus himself as to the genesis of the *Enchiridion.* In a letter written to Botzhem in 1523 he has this to say:

> The *Enchiridion Militis Christiani* was begun by me nearly thirty years ago when staying in the castle of Tournehem, to which we were driven by the plague which depopulated Paris. The work arose out of the following incident. A common friend of mine and of Blatt's was in the castle — a man whose wife was a lady of singular piety. The husband was no one's enemy so much as his own, a man of dissolute life, but in other respects an agreeable companion. He had no regard for any clergyman except me; and his wife who was much concerned about her husband's salvation, applied to me through Blatt to set down some notes in writing for the purpose of calling him to some sense of religion, without his perceiving that it was done at the insistence of his wife. For even with her it was a word and a blow, in soldier fashion. I consented to the request and put down some observations suitable to the occasion. These having met with the approval even of learned persons, and especially of Joannes Vitarius, a Franciscan friar of great authority in those parts, I finished the work at leisure, after the plague (then raging everywhere) had routed me out of Paris and driven me to Louvain.[69]

The first edition of the *Enchiridion* was published in 1503

[67] *Ibid.,* p. 57.
[68] *Ibid.,* p. 58.
[69] F. Nichols, *The Epistles of Erasmus* (London, 1910), pp. 337-338.

and indicates that it had been completed in the monastery of Bertinicius at St. Omer in southern Holland. Mann Phillips remarks: "One cannot help regretting that this little book was not first written in a modern European language; it might have ranked beside the early masterpieces of the Renaissance."[70] Between 1514 and 1518 some eight Latin editions of the work appeared. It was translated into English in 1518, into Czech in 1519, German in 1520, Dutch in 1523, Spanish in 1526, French in 1529, Portuguese in 1541, Italian in 1542, and Polish in 1585. There is no question that it was one of the most widely read books of the age. Professor Adrian Barrland at Louvain called it "a booklet of genuine gold" and emphasized its usefulness for everyone, lay or cleric. A renowned preacher at Antwerp recommended it by saying that virtually every page held a sermon. The Bishop of Basel carried it with him continually and once showed it to its author, pointing out that he had underlined sentences on almost every page. The book has exercised a lasting influence in the Church of England even to the present day. The philosophy the work contained modified the tone of Calvinism in the low countries. French Catholics used the book in the seventeenth century to influence their Calvinistic compatriots toward a return to the ancient faith. The *Enchiridion* was carried to the New World by Spanish explorers and native Indians were reading it before the end of the century.

The present translation is based upon the Basil edition of 1518 and the *Erasmi Opera Omnia* of Leclerc (1704). There have been paraphrases and deletions to accommodate the modern reader. It is sincerely hoped that its reading will have the effect aimed at by its author, namely, to make religion for those living in the world a more dynamic thing by "referring all things to Christ."

---

[70] M. Philips, *Erasmus and the Northern Renaissance* (London, 1949), p. 46.

# HANDBOOK
## OF THE
# MILITANT CHRISTIAN

*(Enchiridion Militis Christiani)*

# II

"Non faciat ad disputationem theologicam,
modo faciat ad vitam theologicam."

"Let this book lead to a theological life
rather than theological disputation."
*Letter of Erasmus to Abbott Volz,
August, 1518.*

## I.

You have requested, my dearly beloved in Christ, that I compose for you a kind of compendium, or guide for spiritual living, so that being instructed by it you may attain those virtues of mind that should characterize him who is truly Christian. In this request you have also indicated that your preoccupation with mundane affairs has forced you to perceive the need you have of abandoning worldly pursuits and turning your efforts rather to the attainment of virtue. Our own close friendship only adds to the joy with which I undertake this proposal, and I sincerely hope that He who is solely responsible for your decision will aid me in this endeavor. So that what I have to write will not in the end prove fruitless, let us begin by calling upon the kindly spirit of Jesus so that He will fill my mind with words of salvation, and that what I write will be for you a source of strength and determination.

1. *In this life it is necessary that we be on our guard.*

To begin with we must be constantly aware of the fact that life here below is best described as being a type of continual warfare. This is a fact that Job, that undefeated soldier of vast experience, tells us so plainly. Yet in this matter the great majority of mankind is often deceived, for the world, like some deceitful magician, captivates their minds with seductive blandishments, and as a result most individuals behave as if there had been a cessation of hostilities. They celebrate as if they were assured of victory when, as a matter of fact, genuine peace could never be further away. It is amazing to see in what false security these people live and in what a complacent manner they close their minds to reality. In the meantime the vices, our armored enemies, attack us unceasingly; we are entrapped by their espionage and assaulted with their endless deceptions. If you but look around, you will see that regardless of where you go they are observing you. They are prepared to attack us with a thousand stratagems and, evil demons that they are, they concentrate on wounding our minds with inflammable and poisonous weapons. Unless we ward them off with the impenetrable shield of faith they will prove to wield weapons of certain death. Nor is there any slackening in the manner of their attack, as it comes from all sides.

This is that world that St. John describes so well as being constituted entirely of vice. It is a world that is both contrary and hateful to Christ. It must be pointed out that the type of warfare it wages is anything but simple and straightforward. From time to time, especially in adverse circumstances, this raging world shakes the very walls of the mind. At other times it incites the mind to betrayal with vain promises. Or again, whenever it finds us unaware, in idle and false security, it unexpectedly and with secret contrivances captures the mind. Most important of all, that slimy snake, the first betrayer of our peace and the father of restlessness, never ceases to watch and lie in wait beneath the heel of woman, whom he once poisoned. By "woman" we mean of course the carnal or sensual part of man. For this is our Eve, through whom the crafty serpent entices and lures our minds to deadly pleasures. And yet, as if it were not enough that he threatens us from all directions on the outside, he also penetrates into the inner recesses of our minds. This is the ancient and earthly Adam, more intimate than our closest companions and more zealous than our deadliest enemy, since he cannot be contained by entrenchment or expelled with an army. He must be watched, then, with a hundred eyes, lest he expose God's fortress to demons.

Since it is quite plain that all of us are engaged in a major and difficult effort against an enemy who is numerically superior, better armed, and more experienced than we are, are we not insane if we fail to take up arms against him? Are we not extremely foolish if we do not stand continually on our guard and hold all things suspect? The fact of the matter is, however, that we slumber complacently through the whole siege. Indulgence in pleasure rather than hard work seems to be the norm. The self-interest we display would convince one that we are living in peaceful times. It seems that life is a drinking bout rather than a war. We clothe ourselves with boudoir trappings rather than armor. Ease and self-indulgence are everywhere preferred to the rigors of military preparedness. We practice on the peaceful harp rather than on the weapons of warfare, unaware that this sort of peace is the most terrible of all wars.

Anyone who concludes a treaty with vice violates the agreement made with God in Baptism. You foolishly cry, "peace, peace," and at the same time treat as an enemy God, who alone is peace and the author of peace. He Himself has made it quite plain through His prophet: "There is no peace for the wicked." The condition that He lays down for peace is that we fight in the garrison of the body against all of our vices. If we compromise, if we consort with vice, we will make a foe of Him who alone, as a friend, is able to bless us, but who as an enemy will surely damn us. He will be our enemy for two reasons. First of all we will be siding with those vices which are diametrically opposed to the divine, for how can light and darkness be in agreement? In the second place, in so doing we ungratefully fail to abide by the pledge that we have made to Him, violating what we have solemnized with sacred ceremonies. Perhaps you are not aware, O Christian soldier, that when you were initiated into the mysteries of life-giving Baptism, you gave yourself by name to Christ as your leader. That is the reason you are doubly indebted to Him. He not only gave you life in the first place but He also restored it. You owe Him more than you could ever owe to yourself. If you break this contract does it not occur to you that you are violating a pledge to such a kindly leader? Does it not become quite plain to you that you have dedicated yourself in this sacrament to His most noble cause? Why did He see to it that you were signed on the brow with the sign of the cross unless He intended that you fight under His banner during this life? For what purpose were you anointed with sacred oils except to take up arms in this struggle against vice? What could be more shameful, more degrading, than to separate yourself from this princely leader? Is there any reason why you should hold Christ the King in derision? Does not the fact that He is God at least instill you with fear? Are you not moved by the love of Him who for your sake became man? Has no one ever warned you of the promise you once laid before Him? Will you actually betray Him who once redeemed you with the price of His blood?

Certainly you show the greatest impudence if you dare raise a hostile standard against a King who gave His life for your sake. He Himself has told us clearly that he who does not stand for Him stands against Him, and he who does not gather with Him, scatters. Not only do you fight under a disgraceful banner, but consider for a moment what your reward will be. St. Paul, the standard-bearer of Christian warfare, tells us "the wages of sin is death." Would anyone engage in warfare if death were the only reward? Death of the soul is hardly a reward. Look at the actual condition of misery that accompanies human warfare. What motivates the soldiers to endure such hardships and deprivation? Is it not the promise of booty, the dread of loss, and the fear of being accused of cowardice? If all they get is the praise of their officers, or the hope of a little more pay, that is not much of a reward. Our motives can be neither the fear of shame nor the hope of reward. The same Person witnesses our struggle who will one day reward us. Our reward is that which "neither eye has seen, nor ear heard, nor has entered into the heart of man." I think this in itself ought to be of great consolation as we carry on the battle, for it is eternal happiness that will be ours.

In all earthly engagements a reputation for bravery is the goal, and even the material rewards are handed out by lot. With us in our struggle against vice the case is not quite the same. We do not fight for praise but for Life itself. And the very highest reward will go to him who perseveres, just as the most severe punishment will be meted out to him who deserts. Heaven itself is the promise we seek and certainly the very hope of such a prize ought to encourage our efforts, especially when it is promised by Him who can neither deceive nor be deceived. Then too our struggle takes place before the all-seeing eye of God and is witnessed by the entire populace of heaven. The shame of defeat in the presence of such an audience ought to at least help inspire us to bravery. He will praise our effort whose mere approval alone is the equivalent of the greatest happiness. If the tepid mind is not aroused by the prospect of reward, it must be admitted that fear of punishment can awaken even the most indolent.

In ancient times it was customary, in war, to violate the corpses of the enemy. It was considered a great calamity if the body were separated by the sword from the soul. This enemy of ours is not only determined to destroy the body but he intends to cast both the body and the soul into hell. For this is actually what occurs when life, which is God Himself, is taken away from the soul. We know well enough that it is the nature of the body to eventually perish because, even though no one attempts to kill it, it cannot live on forever. But for the soul to die is another matter and one of extreme misfortune. I do not have to point out to you the great care and solicitude we exercise in caring for the wounds of the body; we doctor them with the greatest of concern. And yet at the same time we woefully neglect the wounds of the soul. All of us are horrified at the sight of a dying body because we are able to witness it with our bodily eyes. Yet since the death of the soul is something we cannot witness, there are very few who believe in it and even fewer who are actually frightened at the thought of it. I might point out that the death of the soul is certainly more frightful than the death of the body. This is evident enough from the fact that the soul is something far greater than the body and God, whose loss it entails, is greater than the soul.

Let me give you some signs, some evidence, whereby you can determine whether or not your soul is diseased or perhaps even dead. If you are troubled with indigestion, if it is difficult to retain food, it is quite apparent that there is something physically wrong with your body. Now the Word of God has been referred to as the food of the soul. If it is unpalatable, if it nauseates you, there can be little doubt that the palate of your soul is infected with diseases. If food is not retained, if it does not proceed along the digestive tract, it is pretty clear that your soul is sick. When your knees totter and it is only with difficulty that you drag your ailing limbs about it is quite evident that you have an ailing body. Now you must certainly have a disease of the soul when the performance of an act of piety is done with great reluctance and hesitancy, when you have no strength to bear up under a slight rebuke, or when the loss of a few pennies makes you troubled and angry. There can be no doubt that after the sight leaves the body, when the ears fail to hear, and the whole body loses its sensitivity, then the soul has departed. When the eyes of the heart are so obscured that you cannot perceive the brightest light (that is, truth), when you are no longer aware with your inner ears of the divine voice, do you think your soul is really alive? You see your brother suffering indignities. Provided your own affairs are not endangered, your mind is not in the least moved. Why at this point does your soul feel absolutely nothing? It certainly must be because it is dead. Why dead? Because God, its very life, is not present. Where God is, there is charity, for God is charity. Otherwise, if you are a living member, how can any part of the body be in pain without your feeling anything?

Let me give you another sign that is even more certain.

Supposing that you have deceived a friend, or that you have committed adultery; in other words, you should have received a major wound, and yet not only are you unaware of any pain but you actually take pleasure in recalling your wickedness. Can there be any doubt that your soul is dead? We generally assume that the body is not alive if it is insensible to the prick of a pin. Can a soul be considered alive if it is unfeeling in this matter? Let us take another example. You happen to be in the company of someone who is using filthy language, who is raging in anger against his neighbor. If you think that his soul is alive, you are deceiving yourself. It is more like a stinking corpse whose foulness infects all who come near it. Christ referred to the Pharisees as whitened sepulchers. Why? Because they carried their dead souls about within themselves. The bodies of holy people are temples of the Holy Spirit. The bodies of evil men are sepulchers of dead corpses. No cadaver is so dead as that soul which has been abandoned by God. And certainly no corpse offends the nostrils of men to the extent that the evil odor of the buried soul offends the sensibility of the heavenly court. When dying words proceed from the heart we can assume that a dead soul lies within. For, according to the saying of the Gospel, "the mouth speaks from the abundance of the heart," and if God, the life of the soul, is present, the soul will speak divine words.

If we read the Gospel we find that the disciples once asked our Lord, "Whither shall we go? You have the words of life." Why "words of life"? The only answer to be found is the fact that these words flowed from a soul that was never for a moment separated from the divinity and which alone restores us to everlasting life. It is not a rare thing that pious men have recalled a dead body to life. But we must never forget that God does not revive a dead soul except by an extraordinary and gratuitous power, and certainly He does not resuscitate it if it is already dead when it leaves the body. I think that we can agree that the sensation of death in the body is very slight or at least it is very brief. The sensation of death in the case of the soul is entirely different; it is more than death itself, because it is everlasting.

With these remarks in mind need I point out further the tremendous powers of our adversary? It would be sheer stupidity not to be aroused to this fearful danger, and to take the necessary precautions against it. On the other hand you must avoid the pitfall of losing courage or feeling unable to cope with the situation. For we must never forget that regardless of the strength of the enemy we have an ever-present and an all-powerful auxiliary. "If God is for us, who is against us?" If He sustains us, what can be lacking? We must be ever inflamed with the hope and conviction of final victory. Let us not forget that our encounter is not with an undefeated enemy but with one who was once broken and who many years ago was overthrown, despoiled, and led captive by Christ our Head. This same Christ will unquestionably subdue him again in us. If we but remember to whose Body we belong, we will triumph in the strength of our Head. No man is strong in his own strength. In Him alone we will find our real worth.

This is the reason why I reiterate that the outcome of this war is not in the least to be doubted. Victory is not something that depends upon chance; it is entirely in the hands of God and, through Him, also in our hands. Anyone who has failed in this struggle was simply lacking in a will to conquer. The kindness of our Leader has never failed anyone. If you but listen to His call and do your part you shall be assured of victory, for not only will He fight alongside you but His very liberality will be imputed to you as merit. At the same time you must thank Him alone for the victory. He alone is immune from sin and He alone first oppressed its tyranny. Yet this victory will not come without your own effort and diligence, for He who said, "Have confidence, I have conquered the world," does not want your confidence to be a matter of complacency. Profiting by His example we will fight as He fought. We must steer a middle course between Scylla and Charybdis, neither acting too presumptuously because we rely too much on divine grace, nor surrendering in despair because we are disheartened by the difficulties of the war.

## 2. *The weapons of Christian warfare.*

I think we can truthfully say that nothing is more important in military training than a thorough knowledge of the weapons to be employed and the nature of the enemy to be encountered. I would add to this that the need for preparedness, of having the weapons close at hand, is also of the utmost importance. In ordinary warfare it is customary that leave of absence or actual retirement to winter quarters brings about a cessation of hostilities from time to time. This is certainly not the case in the kind of warfare we are describing. We can never permit ourselves to be even a finger's length from our weapons. Since our enemy is incessant in his attacks we must be constantly on the battle line, constantly in a state of preparedness. As a matter of fact, our enemy, when he appears peaceful, when he feigns flight or a truce, can at that very moment be assumed to be preparing for an attack. He is most dangerous when he appears peaceful, and it is during his violent attacks that we can actually feel most secure. It is for this reason that our primary concern must be to keep the mind armed. Our enemies are armed for no other purpose than to destroy us; surely we should not be ashamed to take up arms so as not to perish.

We will speak about Christian armor more in detail when we treat that subject later on. Meanwhile I would like to point out briefly two weapons that we should prepare to use in combating the chief vices. These weapons are prayer and knowledge. St. Paul clearly expresses the desire that men be continually armed when he commands us to pray without ceasing. Pure prayer directed to heaven is able to subdue passion, for it is, as it were, a citadel inaccessible to the enemy. Knowledge, or learning, fortifies the mind with salutary precepts and keeps virtue ever before us. These two are inseparable, the former imploring but the latter suggesting what should be prayed for.

St. James tells us that we should pray always for faith and hope, seeking the things of salvation in Jesus' name. We may recall that Christ asked the sons of Zebedee if they really knew what they were praying for. We must always emphasize the dual necessity of both prayer and knowledge. In your flight from sin, imitate Aaron as a model of prayer, and Moses as an example of knowledge of the law. Neither allow your knowledge to lessen nor your prayer to become sterile.

Listen for a moment to what Christ has to say in Matthew's Gospel: "But in praying, do not multiply words, as the Gentiles do; for they think that by saying a great deal, they will be heard. So do not be like them; for your Father knows what you need before you ask Him." And St. Paul condemns ten thousand words spoken with the lips in favor of five uttered in understanding. Moses spoke nothing yet he heard the words, "Why do you call after me?" It is not the loud sound of the mouth, but rather the pleas of an ardent soul that reach the divine ear. Try to let this be a practice with you: When the enemy assaults you and the other vices give you trouble, lift up your mind to heaven and in your faith do not fail to raise up your hands also. Perhaps the best remedy in this matter is to be continually occupied with works of piety so that you will not revert to worldly affairs but to Christ.

You must believe me when I say that there is really no attack from the enemy, or temptation so violent, that a sincere resort to Holy Writ will not easily get rid of it. There is no misfortune so sad that a reading of the Scriptures does not render bearable. Therefore, if you will but dedicate yourself entirely to the study of the Scriptures, if you meditate day and night on the divine law, nothing will ever terrorize you and you will be prepared against any attack of the enemy.

I might also add that a sensible reading of the pagan poets and philosophers is a good preparation for the Christian life. We have the example of St. Basil, who recommends the ancient poets for their natural goodness. Both St. Augustine and St. Jerome followed this method. St. Cyprian has worked wonders in adorning the Scriptures with the literary beauty of the ancients. Of course it is not my intention that you imbibe the bad morals of the pagans along with their literary excellence. I am sure that you will find, nonetheless, many examples in the classics that are conducive to right living. Many of these writers were, of course, very good teachers of ethics. We have the example of Moses who did not spurn the advice of Jethro. These readings mature us and constitute a wonderful preparation for an understanding of the Scriptures. I feel this is quite important, because to break in upon these sacred writings without this preparation is almost sacrilegious. St. Jerome assails the presumption of those who, even though they may be learned in other fields, presume to expatiate on the Bible. You can imagine the audacity of those who, having no preparation whatsoever, try to do the same thing.

We must not persist in clinging to the letter, and the reading of Homer and Virgil will be of no use unless we look to its allegorical side. If you like the classics then you will understand what I mean. If the obscene passages in the ancients bother you, then by all means refrain from reading them. Of all the philosophical writings I would recommend the Platonists most highly. For not only their ideas but their very mode of expression approaches that of the Gospels. Of course they should be read in a cursory manner and whatever is of real value in them should be applied and referred to Christ. If to the pure of heart all things are clean, then to the impure everything appears to be unclean. Whenever the reading of secular selections arouses your baser appetites, then leave them alone.

Reading the Scriptures with a clean heart is a basic rule. It prevents what is intended to be medicinal from becoming noxious. You must maintain at all times a high regard for the revealed word. It is genuine because it has its origin in the very mind of God. If in all humility and with regulated caution you approach the Scriptures, you will perceive that you have been breathed upon by the Holy Will. It will bring about a transformation that is impossible to describe. You will perceive the delights of the Blessed Bridegroom; you will see the riches of Solomon. The hidden treasures of eternal wisdom will be yours. Yet I would caution you. The entrance to this abode of wisdom is narrow. The doorway is low and there is danger in not stooping when you enter. There is nothing that you can believe with greater certitude than what you read in these writings. The senses themselves cannot offer greater certainty. Divine revelation has made it clear that heaven and earth will not pass away before all that is contained therein is fulfilled. Man may lie and make mistakes; the truth of God neither deceives nor is deceived.

Let me mention another requirement for a better understanding of Holy Scripture. I would suggest that you read those commentators who do not stick so closely to the literal sense. The ones I would recommend most highly after St. Paul himself are Origen, Ambrose, Jerome, and Augustine. Too many of our modern theologians are prone to a literal interpretation, which they subtly misconstrue. They do not delve into the mysteries, and act as if St. Paul were not speaking the truth when he says that our law is spiritual. There are some of these theologians who are so completely taken up with these human commentators that they relegate what the Fathers had to say to the realm of dreams. They are so entranced with the writings of Duns Scotus that, without ever having read the Scriptures, they believe themselves to be competent theologians. I care not how subtle their distinctions are; they are certainly not the final word on what pertains to the Holy Spirit.

If your interest in sacred doctrine revolves more about what is vital and dynamic rather than merely dialectical, if you incline more towards what moves the inner man than to what leads to empty arguments, then read the Fathers. Their deep piety has withstood the test of time. Their very thoughts constitute a prayerful meditation and they penetrate into the very depths of the mysteries they propound. I do not mean to condemn modern theologians, but I am merely pointing out that in view of our purpose, namely, a more practical piety, they are hardly to be recommended. Let us not forget that the Divine Spirit has its own manner of speaking and its own figures of speech. Learn these from the very outset. The Divine Wisdom speaks to us and, like an attentive mother, adjusts Her language to our infancy. For the tiny infants She provides milk and for the sick, herbs. To receive solid food you must grow up spiritually. She lowers Herself to your humility. You must raise yourself to Her sublimity. To remain like an infant is unfortunate. Unending illness is reprehensible. Pluck the marrow from the broken bone: meditation upon a single verse gives more nourishment, brings more wisdom, than continued verbal repetition of the whole psalm.

I warn you with the more diligence because I know that this error has confused not merely the crowd but also those who in name and in garb claim perfect religion. These people believe the greatest piety is repeating as many psalms as possible every day, though they scarcely understand them. On every side monastic piety grows cold, languishes, and disappears because the monks grow old and gray in the letter of the Scriptures rather than maturing to a spiritual understanding. They fail to hear Christ proclaiming in the Gospel: "The flesh profits nothing, it is the spirit that gives life." Nor do they hear Paul adding to the Master's words: "The letter kills, but the spirit brings life." We know the law is spiritual. Spiritual things should not be made carnal. In times past the Father was worshipped in the mountains. Now He wants to be worshipped in the spirit.

I do not want to be misunderstood. I by no means despise the weakness of those who, from feebleness of mind, do the only things they are able to do. Certain words in magic rituals are thought efficacious even when those who pronounce them do so without understanding them. Likewise, divine words, though little understood, should be believed beneficial for those who speak or hear them in sincere faith and pure affection. The angels who are present bring assistance. Nor indeed does Paul condemn those who sing in the spirit or those who speak in tongues. But he does urge a fuller use of graces. Of course, there is no shame for those prevented from better things by vice, not of the mind, but of nature. As St. Paul has said: "Let not him who eats despise him who does not eat; and let not him who does not eat judge him who eats."

However, I do not want you who are better endowed to remain content with the barren letter. Rather I want you to pass on to the more profound mysteries. Strengthen yourselves with frequent prayer, until He who holds the key of David, who closes and no one opens, will open for you the book sealed with the seven seals — the secrets of the Father, which no one knows except the Son, and he to whom the Son deigns to reveal them.

But how should you pray? I intended to describe a way of life, not a method of learning. Yet, I deviated a bit to point out an arsenal of weapons which you could profitably use in this new type of warfare. So pick out from pagan books whatever is best. Follow, in studying the ancients, the example of the bee flying about the garden. Like the bee, suck out only what is wholesome and sweet; reject what is useless and poisonous. Follow this rule, and your mind will be better clothed. Then you will enter into the battle of daily life better armed. Nonetheless, whenever you find truth and virtue, refer it to Christ. If you wish to consult the treasure-house of Paul, that valiant captain, there you will discover "that the weapons of our warfare are not of the flesh, but are mighty before God for the destruction of fortifications, destroying counsels and every height which tends to bar the knowledge of God." You will find the weapons of God by which you can endure an evil day. On your right you will find the arms of justice, on your left the armor of truth, the breastplate of justice, and the shield of faith, a shield with which you can ward off the fiery darts of the devil. You will find also the helmet of salvation, and the sword of the spirit which is the word of God. Carefully fortified with these weapons, a man can fearlessly utter those courageous words of Paul: "Who shall separate us from the love of Christ? Shall tribulation, or distress, or famine, or peril, or persecution, or the sword?" See the many enemies the devil directs, and how frightened they are at everything. But hear something stronger. Paul adds: "But in all these things we conquer because of Him who has loved us. For I am sure that neither death, nor life, nor angels, nor principalities, nor powers, nor things present, nor any other creatures shall be able to separate us from the love of God which is in Christ Jesus." What a happy confidence the arms of light give to Paul, an insignificant man who called himself a castoff of the world!

But to return to our original purpose. We must forge a handy weapon, an *enchiridion,* a dagger, that you can always carry with you. You must be on guard when you eat or sleep, even when you travel in the course of worldly concerns and perhaps become weary of bearing this righteous armor. Never allow yourself to be totally disarmed, even for a moment, lest your wily foe oppress you. Do not be ashamed to carry this little sword with you. For it is neither a hardship to bear nor useless for defending yourself. Though it is a small weapon, it will enable you, if you use it skillfully, to withstand the enemy's tumultuous assaults quite easily and avoid a deadly wound. Now is the time for us to teach ourselves a kind of "manual of arms." I promise that, if you diligently train yourself in it, our sovereign Lord, Jesus Christ, will transfer you, rejoicing and victorious, from this garrison to the city of Jerusalem, where there is neither tumult nor war at all, but everlasting peace and perfect tranquillity. Meanwhile, all hope of safety should be placed in your arms and your armor.

3. *The crown of wisdom is that you know yourself;*
*and of the two sorts of wisdom, false and true.*

Peace is the highest good to which even the lovers of the world turn all their efforts. However, as has been said, their peace is a false one. It is this same sort of peace that the philosophers promise to those who follow their teachings. Christ alone grants that peace which the world cannot give. There is but one way to attain it: we must wage war with ourselves.

We must contend fiercely with our vices. God, our peace, is separated from these enemies by an implacable hatred. His nature is virtue itself. He is the parent and author of all virtue. The dregs drawn from every kind of vice are called folly by the staunchest defenders of virtue, the Stoics. Scripture labels this folly malice. Among all these writers absolute probity is called wisdom. Does not the oracle of the wise man say "wisdom conquers malice"? The father and prince of malice is that ruler of darkness, Belial. Anyone who follows his leadership, walking in the night, hastens to eternal night. On the contrary, the author of wisdom, and Himself Wisdom, Christ Jesus, who is the true Light, alone shatters the night of earthly folly. He is the Splendor of paternal glory, who, as He was made the redemption and justification for us reborn in Him, so also was made Wisdom, as Paul testifies: "We preach Christ crucified, to the Jews a stumbling block, and to the Gentiles foolishness; but to them that are called, both Jews and Greeks, Christ is the Power of God and the Wisdom of God." Through this Wisdom, by His example, we are able to triumph over the malice of the enemy. If we are wise in Him, in Him also shall we conquer. Make the most of this Wisdom. Embrace it! You must set at naught the wisdom of the world which bears a false title and shows itself only to fools. For St. Paul there is no greater foolishness in the sight of God than worldly wisdom; it must be forgotten by him who would be truly wise. If any man among you seems to be wise in this world, let him be known as a fool, for the wisdom of this world is foolishness with God. It is written: "I will destroy the wisdom of the wise, and the prudence of the prudent I will reprove." Where is the wise man, where is the subtle lawyer, where is the searcher of this world? Has not God made the wisdom of this world foolishness?

I doubt not that these wise fools now trouble you hatefully. These blind leaders of the blind shout that you are raving mad. They become hysterical because you are preparing to go over to Christ's side. Merely in name are they Christians. In all other respects they are first mockers and then attackers of

Christ's teachings. Beware lest you be swayed by the blindness of those whose blindness ought to be pitied and deplored rather than imitated. For what is this preposterous kind of wisdom that is so cautious and skillful in worthless things and nothingness? Indeed it is employed for wicked ends. Furthermore, it is no wiser than a dumb beast in those things which alone pertain to our salvation. Paul wishes us to be wise, but in what is good; simple in what is evil. These are wise that they may act evilly; they know not how to be good.

The eloquent Greek poet, Hesiod, judges those who, though they lack wisdom themselves, still refuse to accept good advice to be useless. In what class must we place those who, despite the fact that they are perniciously foolish themselves, never cease to disturb, to mock and to hinder those who have recovered their senses? But shall not the mockers be mocked? He who dwells in the heavens shall mock them, and our Lord shall laugh them to scorn. We read in the Book of Wisdom: "They shall see and shall despise him, but God shall mock them." To be mocked by evil men is, as it were, to be praised. Their worldly wisdom leads inevitably to false presumption which is followed by blindness of the mind, slavery to base appetites, and all other species of vice. The bad habits developed in this manner produce a dullness or insensibility of the mind and the victim no longer considers himself a sinner. The climax of this gradual process of degradation is a sudden and un-provided-for death which is followed by death everlasting.

But of the wisdom of Christ, which the world considers foolishness, we read: "All good things came to me together with her, and innumerable honors came to me through her hands. And I rejoiced in all of these for this wisdom went before me and I knew not that she was the mother of them all." She brings as her companions modesty and gentleness. Gentleness enables you to receive the divine Spirit, for the Spirit rejoices to rest upon a humble and gentle person. While there, it will imbue your minds with its sevenfold grace; it will produce an abundant crop of virtues which will bear blessed fruits —

especially that inner or secret joy which is known only to those who have experienced it and which, in the end, neither vanishes nor is destroyed, but is gathered up into eternal joy. My brother, you ought, in accordance with James' admonition, to seek this wisdom from God with the most ardent intentions and, according to a certain wise man, to "dig it out" from the veins of Divine Scripture "like treasures."

The crown of this God-given wisdom is to know yourself, a maxim which the ancients believed sent from heaven, and in which the great authors took enormous delight, holding it to epitomize the fullness of wisdom. However, let even this have little weight among you if it does not agree with Scripture. The mystical lover in Canticles threatens his bride, ordering her to depart unless she know herself: "If you know not yourself, O beautiful among women, go forth and follow after the sheep of your flock." No one should hold the fantastic opinion that he knows himself well enough. Might I not also question whether anyone knows his body completely or, indeed, whether anyone will truly recognize a habit of mind? Even Paul, whom God so loved that He revealed to him the mysteries of the third heaven, dared not judge himself. He would have undoubtedly have done so if he had known himself well enough. If such a man, a man so spiritual that he could judge all things without himself being judged by anyone, knew himself so little, in what are we carnal folk to put our faith? Surely a soldier who knows neither his own forces nor those of the enemy is quite useless. Yet our war is not between man and man, but within ourselves: the hostile battle lines spring forth in opposition to us from our very flesh itself. A friend is distinguished from an enemy by such a fine line that there is great danger of inadvertently defending an enemy as a friend, or attacking a friend thinking him to be an enemy. Our notorious enemy always takes on the appearance of an angel of light. We need always ask: "Are you one of ours, or one of our adversaries?" Since you must war with yourself and since the first hope of victory lies in whether you know yourself as much as possible, I shall now put before you a kind of likeness of yourself so that you may plainly know what is within and what is merely skin-deep.

### 4. *Of the outer and inner man.*

Man is a very complex creature composed of several contending parts: a soul which may be likened to a sort of divine will, and a body comparable to a dumb beast. In so far as the body is concerned we do not surpass the dumb beasts; indeed, we are inferior to them in every bodily endowment. In regard to the soul we are capable of divinity, that is, we may climb in flight above the minds of the very angels themselves and become one with God. If you did not possess a body, you would be but a spirit; if you were not endowed with a mind, you would be but a beast. The greatest craftsman of all has joined together in happy concord these two diverse natures, but the serpent, hating peace, has split them in unhappy discord. Now they can neither be separated without the greatest suffering nor live together without constant war. Either of these natures might well say to the other, "I cannot live either with you or without you." To such an extent do they contend with one another that one would think that they were utterly incompatible, but they are, in reality, one. Inasmuch as the body is itself visible, it delights in things visible; inasmuch as it is mortal, it follows things temporal; inasmuch as it is heavy, it sinks downward. On the contrary, the soul, mindful of its celestial nature, struggles strenuously against the weight of the earthly body to press upward. It distrusts things seen because it knows such things to be transient. It seeks only those things which are true and everlasting. The immortal loves things immortal; the heavenly, things heavenly. Like takes to like unless it be too deeply immersed in the sordid things of the body. The resulting contagion may cause it to lose its natural gentleness. Neither the fabled Prometheus nor nature itself has implanted this discord, but sin, evilly corrupting what has been well founded, has sown the poisonous seeds of dissension between these two natures which formerly dwelt together in peace. In the past the mind commanded the body without trouble, and the body obeyed freely and willingly. Now, with the natural order of things disturbed, the passions of the body seek to override the reason, and reason is compelled, in a sense, to foresake its direction.

Man, hampered as he is by this perplexing division, may be compared to an unruly state. Such a state is composed of various sorts of men whose dissensions create frequent disturbances and factions. To prevent strife, the greatest power must be given to one supreme authority, and this authority must be of such a nature that it commands nothing that is not for the welfare of the state. To this end it is necessary for him who is wiser to govern, while he who is less wise ought to obey. No one is more lacking in sense than the lower classes, and, for this reason, they should obey the magistrate and not hold office themselves. The king, it is true, should consult the nobility, or the greater by birth, but the final decision must remain in his hands. He should sometimes be warned, but he should never allow himself to be forced or led.

In man reason discharges the office of king. His nobles may be considered to be certain bodily, but not brute, affections. These include: true piety toward parents, charity toward brothers, benevolence toward friends, compassion for those who are afflicted, fear of dishonor, desire for an honest reputation, and like qualities. Consider the dregs of the lower classes to be those affections or passions which dissent as much as possible from the decrees of reason, and which are least humble. These are lust, lechery, envy, and similar diseases of the mind which we ought to resist as overseers restrain dirty, vile slaves so as to ensure that they perform the tasks assigned them by the master, or, at least, so as to prevent them from doing harm. The divinely inspired Plato wrote of all these things in his *Timaeus*.

The proper endowments of kings are: first, that they be as wise as possible so that they do not go amiss through error or lack of knowledge; then, that they do only those things which they know to be good and right and that they do not will, falsely and corruptly, anything which is contrary to the dictates of reason. Whoever lacks either of these two qualities judge to be not a king but a usurper.

### 5. *Of the diversity of passions.*

Though our king, reason, may at times be oppressed, he cannot be corrupted without protesting. He will be able to recover because of the eternal law which has been divinely engraven upon him. If the rest of the common people will obey him, he will do nothing either pernicious or which should be repented. He will do all things with the greatest moderation and the greatest calmness. While the Stoics and the Peripatetics disagree on the subject of the affections, they both agree that we should be guided by reason rather than by passion. The Stoics believe that, when those passions which are most closely connected with the senses have educated you to the point of being able to discriminate between what is to be avoided and what is to be sought, then those passions are to be discarded. They not only regard them as useless for the further pursuit of knowledge, but they consider them to be actually pernicious. For this reason they contend that the truly wise man must be free of all passions of this sort as diseases of the mind. Indeed, they scarcely wish to concede to the perfectly wise man those primary and more human impulses which precede the reason and which they call fantasies. On this point the Peripatetics disagree: they teach that the passions are not to be completely destroyed but merely subdued, for they consider them to be of value as incentive to virtue. Thus, they regard anger as the incentive to fortitude, and envy the incentive to industry. Socrates, in the *Phaedo* of Plato, appears to agree with the Stoics when he says that philosophy is nothing more than a meditation upon death, that is, a withdrawal of the mind, as much as possible, from corporal and sensible things, and a dedication to those things that can be perceived only by reason.

Therefore, it is fitting, first, that we come to recognize the inclinations of the mind, and then, that we realize that none of them is so violent that it cannot be restrained by reason or redirected toward virtue. Everywhere I hear the harmful opinion that men are compelled to vice. And there are others who, because of their ignorance of their own natures, follow those passions believing them to be the precepts of reason. Because anger or envy has prompted them, they think they have acted from zeal for God. As one state is more strife-ridden than another, so too is one person more prone to virtue than another. However, this difference proceeds, not from any mental differences, but either from the influence of heavenly bodies, or from their ancestors, or from their upbringing, or from the complexion of the body itself. Socrates' fable of the good and bad charioteers and the good and bad horses is no old wives' tale. There are some who are born with such a moderate temper and who are so easy to get along with that they incline toward virtue without any virtue at all. They even seem to hurry on of their own accord without any prodding whatsoever. For others, the rebellious body can scarcely be subdued with the roughest rein, goad, or spur, so like to a ferocious, untamed, bucking horse is it. If such happens to be your lot, do not immediately abandon the struggle, but persevere with greater determination. Convince yourself, not that the path of virtue is closed to you, but that a richer means of virtue has been offered you. If, instead, you are endowed with a gentle mind, do not consider yourself to be better than another. You are merely more fortunate, and more fortunate in such a way that you are under greater obligation. Furthermore, who is so fortunate in disposition that there are not a great many things in which he needs to struggle?

Therefore, reason must especially guard that in which one feels most vulnerable. Certain vices appear to be most characteristic of certain nations. Thus, deceit is a common vice among some people, gluttony among others, and lechery among still others. These vices accompany certain bodily habits, as for example, effeminacy and love of pleasure with the sanguine;

anger, ferocity, and evil tongues with the quick-tempered; inactivity and sluggishness with the phlegmatic; envy, sadness, and bitterness with the melancholic. Some of these passions either slacken or increase with age. For example, in youth there is lust, prodigality, and rashness, while in old age there is niggardliness, moroseness, and avarice. There are also passions which seem to be related to sex. For example, men are characterized by ferocity; women by vanity and desire for revenge. Meanwhile, nature, as if to make amends, compensates certain diseases of the mind with certain virtues. Thus, this person is prone to pleasure, but, at the same time, he is not at all irascible or envious; another person is of uncorrupted modesty, but is prouder, more irascible and more worldly. Nor is there any lack of those who are troubled by such great and fatal vices as theft, sacrilege, and homicide. Every effort must be made to combat these, and a firm wall of definite purpose must be built against their exertions. On the other hand, there are certain passions which are so similar to virtue that there is danger lest we be deceived by the doubtful distinction between them. These ought to be corrected in such a manner as to turn them toward the nearby virtue. To give an example, a person who is quite irascible should throw a rein over his mind, and he will be eager, not the least bit sluggish, and he will walk erect. He will be free and simple. Another person is somewhat grasping; let him exercise his reason and he will be frugal. Let him who is inflexible become constant. Let him who is sad become serious-minded. Let him who is tactless become courteous. Other light diseases of the mind should be directed to similar ends. However, we must be on our guard lest we cloak a vice of nature with the name of a virtue, calling sadness gravity, harshness justice, envy zeal, niggardliness thrift, adulation friendship, scurrility urbanity.

This, then, is the only road to happiness: first, know yourself; second, do not allow yourself to be led by the passions, but submit all things to the judgment of the reason. Be sane and let reason be wise, that is, let it gaze upon decent things.

You say that it is difficult to put this advice into practice. Who denies it? Plato has a fitting saying: "Those things which are beautiful are also difficult." Nothing is harder than for a man to conquer himself, but there is no greater reward or blessing. St. Jerome expresses this thought very clearly, just as he does all others. No one is happier than the Christian to whom is promised the Kingdom of Heaven. No one is more burdened than he who must fear for his life every day. No one is stronger than he who conquers the devil. No one is weaker than he who is overcome by the desires of the flesh. If you carefully weigh your own strength, you will say that there is nothing more difficult than to subject the flesh to the spirit; but, if you are mindful of God as your helper, there is nothing easier. Assume a perfect life as your goal; having done so, pursue it in a spirit of determination. The human mind has never strongly commanded itself to do anything which it has failed to accomplish. One of the most essential elements of Christianity is a willingness to be and to act as a Christian. This rule of conduct may appear to be too difficult to accomplish at first, but, in the process of time, it will become easy and, with persistence, actually a pleasure. As the poet Hesiod declares: "The way of virtue is difficult at first, but after you have arrived at the summit there is perfect tranquillity." There is no beast so ferocious that he cannot be tamed by human effort. Can it be that there is no power to tame that agent which is the tamer of all things? In order to train the body you are able to abstain from over-indulgence in drink and to give up the company of women for certain periods of time. Why, then, can you not sacrifice a few months to gain control of your evil inclinations? You must do all things necessary to save your body, as well as your soul, from eternal death.

6. *Of the inner and outer man and his two parts as found in Holy Scripture.*

It is always a great source of embarrassment to me to realize that the great majority of those who bear the name Christian act for the most part as if they were dumb beasts. Most of them are such slaves to their baser appetites that in this spiritual combat they are unable to distinguish between the dictates of reason and the promptings of passion. They actually believe that they are behaving in a reasonable manner so long as they act upon what they feel or see. In fact, they consider that alone to have existence which is perceptible to the senses. Their only criterion for right or wrong is that which appeals to their desires. What they mean by peace is in reality a deplorable state of servitude. Entirely bereft of reason they follow heedlessly wherever their selfish interests lead. This is that false and unhappy peace which Christ, the Author of peace, who will one day reward us, has come to do away with. He accomplishes this by stirring up a wholesome war between father and son, husband and wife, and between those things which weak arguments have attempted to reconcile.

I think it is agreed that the authority of the philosophers rests upon the fact that they state what is contained in a different manner in the Scriptures. What the philosophers term "reason" St. Paul calls either "the spirit" or "the inner man" or occasionally the "law of the mind." What they refer to as the "passions" he calls "the flesh," "the body," "the outer man," or "the law of the members." He says, for example: "Walk in the Spirit, and you shall not fulfill the lusts of the flesh. For the flesh lusts against the Spirit, and the Spirit against the flesh . . . so that you do not the things you would." And again: "If you live according to the flesh you will die; if however, you mortify the flesh by the spirit, you will live." Certainly this is a new order of things; to seek peace in war, war in peace, life in death, death in life, freedom in slavery, slavery in freedom. Listen to what Paul says of freedom: "But if you are led by the Spirit, you are not under the law. We have not received the spirit of bondage again in fear, but you have received the spirit of adoption, as sons of God." We read also in St. Paul concerning "the outer man who is corrupt and the inner man who is renewed from day to day." Plato distinguished two souls in one man. Paul in the same way describes two men so joined in one that both of them will be together in eternal glory or eternal damnation. They cannot be separated. The death of one cannot be the life of the other. What Paul writes to the Corinthians is, I believe, also pertinent: "The first came from the earth and is terrestrial. The second came from heaven and is celestial." And to make this even more clear he applies this duality not only to Christ and to Adam but to ourselves as well. "As was the earthy man, such also are the earthy; and as is the heavenly man, such also are the heavenly. Therefore, even as we have borne the likeness of the earthy, let us bear also the likeness of the heavenly. This I say brethren, because flesh and blood can obtain no part of the kingdom of God, neither will corruption have any part in incorruption."

I think you can see how evident it is that Paul, who elsewhere spoke of the "flesh" and the "outer or corruptible man" here calls him the "earthly Adam." This is certainly the "body of death" about which Paul so frequently speaks. "Unhappy man that I am, who will deliver me from the body of this death?" Pointing out a far different fruit of the flesh and spirit, he writes elsewhere: "For he who sows in the flesh will also reap corruption but he who sows in the Spirit will reap life everlasting." We know that a messenger of Satan came to trouble Paul in the flesh. When the tempter refused to leave him, God gave him this answer: "Paul, my grace is sufficient for thee." For strength is made perfect in weakness. This certainly is a new sort of remedy. Lest Paul be proud, he is tempted by pride. That he might be made firm in Christ, he is forced to be infirm. For he carried the treasure of heavenly revelations in a vessel of clay, that the sublimity might reflect the power of God, and not his own power. There are of course many other examples in the writings of St. Paul that indicate how we are to overcome temptation. Our first recourse in any kind of temptation is to implore the assistance of Almighty God. In fact those who are well advanced on the road to perfection will actually welcome these temptations for they guard virtue and, especially, form a bulwark against the danger of vanity which often lurks in the midst of the virtues. We might compare this vanity to the Herculean hydra because it is so difficult to destroy. Let us follow the example of the holy patriarch Jacob in this struggle against sin. He teaches us to persevere during the dark night of struggle until the dawn of divine assistance shines forth. Like him let us say to God "I will not let go until you bless me. . . ." The reward that this great wrestler with evil obtained contains a message for all of us. In the first place God blessed him on the very spot. This shows that after we overcome a temptation graces are immediately granted us so that we can resist the next attack. Furthermore we read that God and the angel then smote Jacob so that henceforth he was lame in one foot. This was, of course, to show that God curses those who attempt to serve two masters. From that time on Jacob walked only on the right foot, that is to say he walked in the spirit. Even his name was changed and from a highly active person he was transformed into a contemplative. In like manner, after you have overcome temptation and crucified your flesh with its evil desires, you will find true peace and tranquillity, and you will see that the Lord is sweet. God is never perceived in the midst of temptation, but once the tempest subsides we will bask in the sunshine of spiritual consolation. Examine yourself in all honesty. If you are flesh alone, you will not see God, you will not be saved. Make it your determined effort then, to become spiritual.

### 7. *Of the three parts of man: spirit, soul and flesh.*

In order to carry this comparison a bit further and to investigate it more fully, let us briefly refer to Origen and his treatment of the nature of man. Following St. Paul and those prophets of the Old Testament, Isaiah and Daniel, Origen speaks of a threefold division in man. The body or flesh is our lowest part. Satan, because of the original transgression has,

as it were, inscribed upon this part the law of sin whereby we
are inclined to evil. Failure to overcome this inclination brings
us completely under his control. The spirit, on the other hand,
may be said to represent us as a reflection of the divine nature
of our Creator. Here we find the original pattern of the divine
mind wherein the eternal law is engraved by the finger of God,
the Holy Spirit. This is that part of us that binds us to God
and makes us one with Him. Finally there is the third part,
resting between the other two, which makes us partakers of the
world of natural sensibilities and impulses. This Origen terms
the soul.

I would like to describe the relation of the soul to the other
two faculties by using the metaphor of a civil disturbance within
a state or commonwealth. The soul is like a country involved
in a political upheaval, seditious and revolutionary. Disinclined
to ally itself with the other two parts, it is nevertheless at liberty
to join one or the other. If by renouncing the flesh it decides
to join itself to the spiritual faction, it will become spiritual.
But if it goes over to the side of the flesh then it must be considered as belonging to the body or the lowest component.
St. Paul in his Epistle to the Corinthians brings out this very
point: "Do you not know that he who cleaves to a harlot
becomes one body with her, but he who cleaves to the Lord
is one spirit with Him?" The expression "harlot" refers of
course to the weaker nature of man in the same sense that
the second chapter of Proverbs uses the term "woman": "That
you may be liberated from the strange woman and from the
stranger who softens her words and has forgotten the guide of
her youth and the covenant of her God, for her house inclines
unto death and her paths to hell. Whatever goes into hell shall
not return, and shall not attain the way of life." Again in the
sixth chapter we read: "That you may keep yourself from the
evil woman and the flattering tongue of the stranger, let not
your heart covet her beauty. Do not be deceived by her beckon-
ings, for the price of a harlot is hardly worth the price of a
loaf of bread. The woman takes away the precious soul of man."

For "whoever is joined to her shall descend into hell, and whoever shall depart from her shall be saved." It seems to me that there could not be a better description anywhere of the poison of sensual pleasure or of the terrible fate of those who live according to the flesh.

Let me sum up how we distinguish these various components of man. The spirit has the capacity of making us divine; the flesh tends to bring out our animal nature; the soul is what really constitutes us as human beings. It is the spirit that gives us the qualities of religion, obedience, kindness, and mercy. The flesh makes us despisers of God, disobedient and cruel. The soul, on the other hand, is indifferent, neither good nor bad in itself. Let me now show you how this threefold tendency operates in actual life. You respect your parents, you love members of your own family, your friends. Certainly we cannot honestly say that there is any real virtue in this. Yet not to do so would immediately be condemned as evil. Even those who are not Christians are expected to love those who are near and dear to them. This is found in the very nature of things and can hardly be imputed to meritorious action. But take a situation where reverence towards parents, or love of children, must be sacrificed for the love of God. Here the soul finds itself torn in two directions. The flesh beckons in one direction, the spirit cries out in the other. The spirit argues that you must obey God as you owe Him all you have. The flesh will answer: "If you disobey your father he will disinherit you, you will be accused of disrespect and lose your good name. Besides God will not notice this and if He does you can be later reconciled with Him." The soul begins to waver. If holding the spirit in contempt she turns to the harlot, that is to the flesh, she will be one body with it. On the other hand, if spurning the flesh, she rises to the spirit, she will be transformed into the spirit alone. How would you act in like circumstances?

I think it is a great mistake indeed to call virtuous those actions which proceed entirely from natural inclinations. There are even certain passions that some mistake for virtue. Take a judge, for example, who condemns a felon simply because this gives him a feeling of self-righteousness. Can you say that he acts in a virtuous way? If he upholds the law for his own evil purposes, for financial gain or personal reputation, his condemnation of the prisoner is tantamount to murder. If, on the other hand, his treatment of the criminal is motivated by personal concern and genuine equity, he acts according to the spirit. I feel that entirely too many people mistake what are really natural gifts or endowments with virtues. You will find that certain individuals are not in the least bothered by temptations of the flesh. Actually this is an indifferent matter. We can speak of virtue in this regard only in the overcoming of an evil inclination. There are some people, too, who get a great deal of consolation out of attending divine services, Mass, vespers, and novenas. If they do this merely because they find pleasure in the ceremonies, because it is emotionally pleasurable or because it enhances their reputation, then they ought to examine their motives. They are in great danger of deceiving themselves. How many there are who, while in the very act of praying, pass judgment on those who are not naturally prayerful. Or again, in the matter of fast and abstinence, what virtue is there if, while you fast, you mentally condemn someone who fails to observe this regulation?

Too many feel that whoever does not carry out the same religious practices as they do is spiritually inferior. Take, for example, a case where your brother is in dire need of your help, and yet you go on mumbling your prayers, pretending not to notice his predicament. God will actually despise that kind of prayer. For how can He possibly listen to your petition while you cannot find it in your heart to help a fellow man? Take another example: You say that you love your wife simply because she is your spouse. There is really no merit in this. Even the pagans do this and the love can be based upon physical pleasure alone. But, on the other hand, if you love her because in her you see the image of Christ, because you perceive in her His reverence, modesty and purity, then you do not love her in herself but in Christ. You love Christ in her. This is what we mean by spiritual love and we will say more about it later on.

## II.

### *Some General Rules For Living a Christian Life.*

Since we now have a general idea of what is to be accomplished by this little treatise, let us proceed lest this become a voluminous tome rather than a manual. It is my plan to propose a number of fundamental rules or norms that will guide us through the labyrinth of this world into the pure light of the spiritual life. If every other science has its own rules then certainly the art of pious living must have some basic regulations. Leading a virtuous life is accompanied by a certain discipline which the Holy Spirit breathes into those who sincerely aim at godliness. Yet I feel that a certain predisposition is necessary, for a refusal to be willing to accept direction is a refusal of God's mercy.

The rules that I will suggest will be garnered from several sources, partly from the Person of God Himself, partly from the devil, and partly from ourselves. They will consist in an enumeration of both virtues and vices as well as components of these. They will be directed for the most part against the evil vestiges of original sin. For it is plain enough that although Baptism has taken away the original stain, yet the remnants of this former disease remain. They are still with us so that our humility might be preserved and so that they might occasion the increase of virtue. We will call them blindness, the flesh, and infirmity or weakness. It is this blindness which dims our reason, resulting in ignorance. For there is very little of that divine light of God's countenance remaining in us. It was partially obscured by the sin of our first parents, and what remains has been completely enveloped through corrupt upbringing, evil companionship, and sinful habits. It is this blindness that drives us to seek after the worst instead of the best. It is this blindness that clouds our judgment, leading us to a false standard of values. It is the flesh that, through our passions, prompts us to cherish what is wrong, even though we know better. Weakness causes us either through tediousness or temptation to lose what virtue we may have already acquired. Blindness harms the judgment, the flesh weakens our will, and weakness destroys our constancy.

To counteract these three vestiges of original sin, I would propose the following: First of all, to combat blindness we must develop a fine sense of discernment by investigating those things that are to be avoided. The flesh will be overcome if we immediately reject evil thoughts and desires and turn our thoughts to what is of God. Finally, we must acquire the habit of perseverance, so that abandoning the pursuit of virtue may appear to us more evil than never having pursued it. Ignorance must be remedied to give us a proper perspective. The flesh must be subdued lest it lead us from the straight and narrow into the alluring path of vice. And last of all, our weakness must be ever strengthened, so that once putting our hand to the plough we refrain from looking back, and advance like a giant, rejoicing until we receive the crown promised to those who persevere.

### The First Rule.

Now since faith is the only gateway to Christ, the first rule I would lay down is that we ought to place great reliance on the Scriptures. This belief should not be, as is the case with most Christians, something cold, careless, and calculated, but rather should come from a fullness of heart. Be convinced that there is not a single item contained in Holy Writ that does not pertain to your salvation. The fact that the majority of mankind considers heaven and hell as some kind of legend or old wives' tale ought not to disturb you. Even if the entire world appear mad, even though the angels revolt and the very elements change, the truth cannot lie. What God has foretold must inevitably take place.

If you believe God exists, then you must believe that He speaks the truth. Convince yourself that nothing you perceive with your senses is as true as what you read in the Scriptures. The will of heaven, Truth Itself, has inspired it; the prophets of old have made it known; the blood of martyrs has proven it; and the constant belief of countless generations has testified to it. Christ Himself in His life here below has exemplified its pervading truth. Even the demons have confessed its veracity since they believe in it just as much as they fear it. Certainly the very beauty of the message it contains should in itself convince anyone who reads it. If such be the case would it not be sheer madness not to believe? Take, for example, the many incredible things that were foretold by the prophets concerning Christ. Not one of them has not taken place. Do you think for a moment that He who did not deceive them would try to deceive others? If these prophets did not lie, certainly Christ, the greatest of all prophets, did not deceive us.

If, convinced of these truths, you ask God to increase your faith, it will indeed amaze me if you do not recoil from an evil life. I think anyone would change his life if he saw the eternal punishment and the torture of a guilty conscience that followed upon sin. Who could possibly exchange the joys of a clear conscience and the anticipation of an eternal reward for a moment of fleeting pleasure?

### Second Rule.

If our first rule demands that we doubt nothing in the divine promises, the second is that we act upon these promises without delay and hesitation. With resolute purpose we must be prepared to undergo loss of everything — property, life itself — for Christ's sake. The kingdom of heaven does not belong to the lazy; it suffers violence and "the violent bear it away."

As you advance on the path to perfection you must determine not to turn back. Neither the affection of your loved ones, the allurements of the world, nor the cares of domestic life should stand in your way. Whenever you cannot disentangle yourself from the affairs and business of the world you must knife your' way through them. The fleshpots of Egypt must be forsaken once and for all. We know what took place when Sodom was not forgotten at once. The woman looked back and was turned to a block of salt; Lot went on into the hills and was saved.

Looking back in this flight from the world will spell immediate defeat. I do not have to point out to you how many there are who delay in their flight from vice. They feel that if they immediately free themselves from this or that business they will not be able to finish it. Let them recall the words: "What if today I should require your soul from you?" I think it is apparent to all that business merely begets more business. One vice merely gives way to another. It is for this reason that I would advise haste in abandoning the world. Do it now — even a little recklessness would not be out of place. Forget about how much you are giving up or what you could have otherwise accomplished and realize that in Christ is the fulfillment of all things. Dedicate yourself to Him with your whole heart. Trust yourself no longer but rather cast yourself entirely into His care. Remember what the prophet said: "The Lord is my Shepherd and I shall not want." You must dare to believe in Him with your whole heart and to distrust yourself entirely. In other words, get out of your own self and let Him support you. Give up this idea of trying to divide yourself between the world and Christ. "You cannot serve two masters." There is no compromise between God and Belial. Never forget for a moment that our God is a jealous lover of souls. He wants all for Himself. And rightly so, for did He not purchase all of us with His blood? Fellowship with Satan is out of the question, as Christ has completely conquered him by His death.

There are only two paths open to you. The one through gratification of the passions, leads to perdition; the other, through mortification of the flesh, leads to life. Which one of these do you choose? There is no third way and sooner or later you will have to make up your mind about one or the other of these. Yet let me remind you that this is a path upon which few men walk and it is a path that you yourself can walk only by exercising the greatest skill. Yet to say that it is beyond our capacities is ridiculous. Christ has trodden this same path and, since the beginning of time, men pleasing to God have traveled it. You know well enough that if you desire to live with Christ, you must be crucified to this world. Then why delude yourself like a fool? Why, in such an all-important matter, are you so prone to self-deception?

There are all kinds of excuses, of course. Some will say: "I am a secular priest; I am obliged to life in the world." Some will reason: "Even though I am a priest, I have not joined a monastic order, I am no monk." They are in for a shock. And of course the monks easily delude themselves. "We do not belong to a strict order. This message is for others." The young, the rich, the generous, those in high positions reply that what was said to the Apostles can have no possible application to them. What a terrible delusion! Does the idea of living in Christ have any meaning at all? If you are in the world you are not in Christ. Of course, if you mean by the world the earth, the sea, the atmosphere, the heavens, then obviously all of us are in the world. But if the world is for you ambition, desire for honor, promotion, or authority, if the world consists of pleasure and lust, then I doubt if you are even a Christian. Christ spoke indifferently to *all* men, that whoever would not take up His cross and follow Him would not and could not be His disciple. If living by His Spirit means nothing to you, then certainly to die with Christ means even less. If to be crucified to this world, to live for God alone, to be buried with Christ, to rise in His glory, have no meaning, then what does? If His humility, poverty, disregard of self, and incessant labors have no meaning, then neither does His kingdom.

It seems to me that nothing could be more lacking in justice than to offer the same reward to everyone while requiring a few to carry out the mandates upon which the reward is based. What could be more ridiculous than to desire to rule jointly with our Head and yet refuse to suffer with Him? Consequently, stop looking about you and trying to flatter yourself by comparison with others. I will grant that to die to sin is a difficult accomplishment. Even few monks ever actually achieve this. And yet at the same time we must agree that this is something that all of us without exception are sworn to do. When you were baptized you took an oath to do just that. To my way of thinking there is no vow or no promise that is more religious or sacred than this. All of us, princes or paupers, are going to stand or fall on this one promise. There is really no other way of salvation. Even though all of us cannot reach this goal, cannot attain the perfect imitation of the Head, all of us must aim for this goal with all our efforts. The honest decision to become a Christian implies that one has already chosen the better part of Christianity.

### Third Rule.

I feel that fear is one of the real obstacles to the pursuit of virtue. This pursuit seems difficult because it involves relinquishing so many things we have come to love and because it demands incessant struggle against those three really formidable elements, the flesh, the devil, and the world. With that in mind I would like to propose a third rule. We must analyze these unfounded fears; when we do, we will find that they are not as bad as they appear. Even if we prescind from the notion of reward, the way of Christ is the most sensible and logical one to follow.

If you take a little time to think it over, it becomes quite apparent that there is no manner of life in this world that is not crowded with difficulties and hardships. Take a man in high political position. No one in his right mind would aspire to such a position, if he were aware of the difficulties that beset such an office. What an endless parade of scraping and bowing to woo the good will of those above you! What an interminable suppression of disdain and concealment of despite for those with whom you must work! Need I mention the vicissitudes of the military life? The risks and dangers encountered by merchants and businessmen are well enough known. Take the state of matrimony. The cares and miseries flowing from domestic difficulties are incredible. Only those who are married can really appreciate and understand how real they are. Regardless of the vocation you may have chosen, there are difficulties on all sides. The life of man is filled from beginning to end with tribulation, and, besides, the virtuous suffer right along with the guilty. If these are the difficulties you fear, you will find that they actually serve to increase your merit. Without virtue, you will have to put up with them anyway, and with greater trouble and no reward at all.

Let us take a look at those who have decided to fight for the world. In the first place, for how many years do they not endure all kinds of hardships and privations? And for what? For fleeting nothings, mainly. And is there any time during this relentless pursuit of pleasure that they can really be said to be hopeful of the outcome? The miseries that they incur are of such a nature that the longer that they pursue false goals the greater is the pain. And what is the end of all this toil and anxiety? Eternal punishment! Now compare this with the life of virtue. To begin with it becomes less and less tedious as we advance, and this increased pleasantness is further enhanced by the hope we have of eternal happiness. In other words the proportionately greater efforts of the wicked lead only to interminable labor, whereas the lighter efforts of the good culminate in eternal rest. The divine assistance offered to those who labor for God not only lightens the load but changes gall to honey. In the way of the world one care only adds to another, one sorrow gives rise to a second, and there is no peace whatever. Christ sums this all up: "Take my yoke upon you and you will find rest for your souls. For my yoke is easy and my burden light." To put it quite briefly, nothing is more pleasurable than a peaceful conscience, nothing more wretched than to have the mind tormented with a bad conscience.

Yet I would like to add that even were the rewards the same and the toil equal in this comparison, would it not be much nobler to fight and work under the banner of Christ than that of Satan? I think that it is quite obviously preferable to suffer a while with Christ than to consort with the devil. No man in his right senses would take up arms, regardless of the reward, for so deceitful a leader. The rigors of the campaign are hardly worth such a fleeting recompense. Besides, can Satan be trusted to pay what he promises? The worry and concern resulting from this distrust would nullify any real anticipation of gain. If you lose in this gamble, you will be doubly miserable, since you were tricked out of what you hoped for, and your whole effort will be a miserable failure. Remember that Christ neither mocks nor is He mocked. When you abandon the world for Christ you do not give anything up, you rather exchange it for something far better. You change silver into gold and rocks into precious gems.

Granted, your friends will be disappointed. Yet you will soon find more pleasant and reliable ones. You will have to give up some of the pleasures of the body, but they are not in the least comparable to those more certain and purer pleasures of the mind. This change will also bring about diminution of your material possessions, but here again what you will gain will be immune from moths and thieves. If your reputation in the world is not what it was, the friendship of Christ will more than make up for this. You will gradually come to realize the transparency of what you once cherished. Even those things which are of themselves quite harmless and licit you will come to regard with indifference. Good fortune usually comes to those who are not looking for it, and certainly if you are attached to absolutely nothing at all, what comes your way will be beneficial. Do not hesitate, then, to give up the devil and seek after Christ. For, regardless of how you estimate the situation, there is absolutely no comparison between the two.

### Fourth Rule.

In order to help you expedite this decision I am going to lay down a fourth rule: Make Christ the only goal of your life. Dedicate to Him all your enthusiasm, all your effort, your leisure as well as your business. And don't look upon Christ as a mere word, an empty expression, but rather as charity, simplicity, patience, and purity — in short, in terms of everything that He has taught us. Consider as the devil, on the other hand, anything that deters us from Christ and His teaching. "When your eye is single, your whole body will be filled with light." Direct your gaze toward Christ alone to the extent that you love nothing, or desire nothing, unless it be either Christ or because of Christ. This way whatever you do, whether you sleep or wake, or eat or drink, or take your leisure, you will increase your reward.

Now since there are many situations where we have to decide whether or not a seemingly indifferent act leads toward or away from Christ, I am going to prescribe a threefold norm to determine our action in just such a situation. There are certain actions that can at no time be considered as other than intrinsically evil. To avenge a wrong, or to desire to injure your neighbor are of this type. These must be shunned at all costs. There are other actions that by their very nature are so virtuous that they can never be really wicked, for example, wishing well to all men, helping friends with honest aid, hating vices, and participating in godly conversation. There are other things that of their very nature are indifferent, morally speaking. Among these we might list health, beauty, strength, eloquence, learning, and the like. Now none of these attributes should be used other than to aim at Christ. They should be evaluated in terms of how adequately they lead to this goal. This should be the criterion upon which we accept or reject them. I would say that among these things knowledge is the most to be valued. I would prefer it to beauty, strength of body, and riches. And although all learning is of great value there is here again a certain priority. If you are interested in learning, certainly this is a fine quality, provided you turn your knowledge to Christ. If, on the other hand, you love letters only for the sake of knowledge, you have not gone far enough. You should go a step further. Let your study bring you to a clearer perception of Christ so that your love for Him will increase and you will in turn be able to communicate this knowledge of Him to others. However, I would admonish you to know your own limitations in this matter.

Of the other attributes I have mentioned I would urge you to use them as the occasion presents, but in such a way that they do not form a hindrance to your spiritual progress. Suppose you come into money. If this does not harm your personal integrity then by all means use it. But if you feel that it may be an occasion for dishonesty, then imitate Crates of old and throw your wealth away. You can do this rather easily if you accustom yourself to admiring nothing that is outside yourself, namely, things that do not pertain to the inner man. This way you will neither grow arrogant if fortune does not smile on you, nor will you be greatly troubled if your wealth is taken away. It will help you in your conviction that Christ alone is the measure of happiness. If you feel that good fortune might be a real hindrance to your progress, then imitate Prometheus and leave the box alone. Anyone who actually admires money as the most precious thing in life, and rests his security on it to the extent of believing that as long as he possesses it he will be happy, has fashioned too many false gods for himself. Too many people put money in the place of Christ, as if it alone has the key to their happiness or unhappiness.

What I say about money also applies to honors, pleasures, health, in fact to the life of the body itself. Our determination to imitate Christ should be of such a nature that we have no time for these matters. St. Paul tells us: "The time is short; it remains that they who enjoy this world be as if not enjoying it." There is no doubt that this sort of reasoning is the object of scorn and derision in the world. Yet this is precisely the type of foolishness with which it has pleased God to protect those who believe. "For the foolishness of God is wiser than men." Let this saying be a guide for your every action. If you are a breadwinner engaged in supporting your family, then this is a noble end in itself. But do not forget that your household must be won over for Christ. Supposing you decide to fast. Certainly this has all the appearance of a virtuous act. But what is the motive for your fasting, to what do you refer it? Is it not perhaps that you might conserve on food? Is it because others will then think you more pious? Most likely you fast in order to preserve your health. And why are your fearful of overeating? For the simple reason that this can interfere with your pursuit of pleasure. Perhaps you are concerned about your health so that you can continue your studies. And why, might I ask, are you so concerned about studies? In order to obtain the easy living of a clergyman, a living that is for your own pleasure and not for Christ's. You have really missed the target towards which every Christian ought to aim. If you eat sufficiently and take care of your health so that you can take part in religious exercises, then you are hitting the mark. If your concern for health and gracious living is only to enable you to be more vigorous in lustful pursuits, you have fallen away from Christ and have made a god out of yourself.

Now there are not a few who are given over to the veneration of the saints, with elaborate ceremonies. Some, for example, have a great devotion to St. Christopher. Provided his statue is in sight, they pray to him almost every day. Why do they do this? It is because they wish to be preserved from a sudden and unprovided death that day. There are others who have a great devotion to St. Roch. Why? Because they believe that Roch can immunize them against certain physical ailments. Others mumble certain prayers to St. Barbara or St. George so they will not fall into the hands of the enemy. Still others fast in honor of St. Apollo so that they will not be troubled with toothaches. Others visit the image of holy Job to prevent boils. There are certain merchants who assign a portion of their profits to the poor so that they will not suffer a loss of merchandise in shipwreck. A candle is burned in honor of St. Jerome so that lost goods might be recovered. In short, for everything we fear or desire, we set up a corresponding deity. This has gone to the extent that each nation has its own. Among the French St. Paul is esteemed, among us Germans St. Jerome has a special place. Certain areas hold St. James or St. John in lesser or greater esteem. This kind of piety, since it does not refer either our fears or desires to Christ, is hardly a Christian practice. As a matter of fact, it is not a great deal different from the superstitions of the ancients. They pledged a tenth of their goods to Hercules that they might get rich, or a cock to Aesculapius to regain their health. A bull was sacrificed to Neptune to avoid mishap at sea. The names may have changed but the purpose and intentions are the same.

You pray that you may not be overtaken by a premature death. Would it not be more Christian to pray that you might be of such a virtuous mind that wherever death overtakes you, it will not find you unprepared? You have absolutely no intention of changing your way of life, and yet you ask God that you may not die. Certainly the only reason you pray is that you may continue your life of sin as long as possible. You pray for the material things of this world and have not the slightest idea of how to use divine things. Are you not actually praying for your own ruin? You pray for good health and yet you continue to abuse it. Is not this rather a dishonoring than an honoring of Almighty God?

I am sure that these remarks will be disturbing to certain so-called saintly men who identify the worship of God with financial gain and who, with their sweet benedictions, deceive the minds of the innocent, serving their own bellies rather than Christ. They will protest that I am forbidding the veneration of the saints in whom God is also honored. I do not damn those who do these things with a simple and childish sort of superstition so much as I do those who, for their own advantage, magnify these practices completely out of proportion. They encourage these devotions, which of themselves are tolerable, for their own profit and thereby capitalize on the ignorance of the masses. What I utterly condemn is the fact that they esteem the indifferent in place of the highest, the nonessentials to the complete neglect of what is essential. What is of the smallest value spiritually they make the greatest. I will certainly praise them for seeking a healthy body from St. Roch, provided they consecrate their life to Christ. But I will praise them still more if they pray for nothing else than a love of virtue and a hatred for vice. As for dying or living, let them leave such matters in the hands of God, and let them say with Paul: "Whether we live, we live unto the Lord; and whether we die, we die unto the Lord." What would be ideal is that they desire to be dissolved from the body and be with Christ. It would be perfect if they, in disease and misfortune, make their real joy consist in this, that they have conformed their lives to Christ their Head. Accordingly, to practice these devotions is not so much to be condemned as is the danger inherent in them, namely, that of relying entirely or too much on them. I suffer from infirmity and weakness, but with St. Paul, I show forth a more excellent way. Examine yourself in the light of these rules and you will not be content with these indifferent actions until all of them are referred to Christ; you will not stop midway but will continue so that all is aimed at serving and honoring God.

### Fifth Rule.

I am now going to add a fifth, subsidiary, rule. You will find that you can best maintain this piety if, turning away from visible things, which are for the most part either imperfect or of themselves indifferent, you seek the invisible. We will follow the divisions we mentioned previously in discussing the nature of man. I am going to stress the difference between the visible and invisible because I find so many Christians, either out of neglect or sheer ignorance, as superstitious as the pagans. Let us suppose that there are two worlds, the one intelligible, the other visible. The intelligible or angelic world is that in which God dwells with the blessed. The visible world embraces the circle of heaven, the planets, the stars, and all that is included in them.

Now let us imagine that man is a third world participating in both of the others, the visible referring to his corporeal part, the invisible to his soul. In the visible world, since we are, as it were, mere sojourners, we ought to consider all that we perceive through our senses in terms of its relationship to the intelligible world. The sun, for example, in the visible world, might be compared to the divine mind. The moon might be thought of in terms of the whole assembly of the angelic hosts and of the elect whom we call the Church Triumphant. These celestial bodies operate in relation to the earth as God does in relation to our soul. It is the sun which quickens, produces, matures, purges, softens, illuminates, brightens, and gladdens. When you are delighted by the beauty of the rising sun, consider the joy of those in heaven upon whom the divine light shines eternally. Paul tells us: "For God, who commanded light to shine out of darkness, has shone in our hearts, to give enlightenment concerning the knowledge of the glory of God, shining on the face of Christ Jesus." I suggest that you repeat over and over those passages from Holy Scripture in which grace is compared to the rays of the sun. If the darkness of night is oppressive to you, then think of how destitute is the soul without the light of God. If you find any darkness within your soul, then pray that the Sun of righteousness may shine upon you.

The things that we can see with our physical eyes are mere shadows of reality. If they appear ugly and ill-formed, then what must be the ugliness of the soul in sin, deprived of all light? The soul, like the body, can undergo transformation in appearance. In sin it appears as completely ugly to the beholder. In virtue it shines resplendently before God. Like the body the soul can be healthy, youthful, and so on. It can undergo pain, thirst, and hunger. In this physical life, that is, in the visible world, we avoid whatever would defile or deform the body; how much more, then, ought we to avoid that which would tarnish the soul? I feel that the entire spiritual life consists in this: that we gradually turn from those things whose appearance is deceptive to those things that are real . . . from the pleasures of the flesh, the honors of the world that are so transitory, to those things that are immutable and everlasting. Socrates had this in mind when he said that the soul will leave the body at the time of death with little fear if, during life, it has rehearsed death by despising material things.

Now the cross to which Christ calls us, and the death in which St. Paul urges us to die with our Head, is of this earth. Once we have tasted the sweetness of what is spiritual, the pleasures of the world will have no attraction for us. If we disregard the shadow of things, then we will penetrate their inner substance. Sickness, for example, can be a means of advancing in spirituality. In fact, a little less care for physical well-being will give us more time to devote to the mind. If you fear the death of the body, then certainly you should fear the death of the soul. If lightening terrifies you, then think of that invisible lightening that is the wrath of God saying: "Depart ye cursed persons into eternal fire." Are you attracted by what is beautiful in the human figure? Think rather of the beauty of the soul that it conceals. You worry whether the drought will end. It is far better that you pray that God may water your mind lest virtue wither away in it. You are greatly concerned with money that is lost or being wasted, or you worry about the advance of old age. I think it much to be desired that you provide first of all for the needs of your soul.

Now this distinction that we make of body and soul can be applied also to what we read in Holy Scripture. Everything that is written has both an external or, as it were, corporeal meaning, as well as a mysterious or spiritual significance. The Old Testament is filled with the accounts of events that would in no way edify us if we did not understand them in an allegorical manner, that is, by searching out the spiritual meaning. St. Paul, following the example of our Lord Himself, has used allegory as a means of better understanding the Scriptures. Origen, of course, is also a great advocate of the allegorical approach. Yet I think you will have to admit that our modern theologians either despise this method of interpretation or are completely ignorant of it. As a matter of fact, they surpass the pagans of antiquity in the subtlety of their distinctions.

I find that in comparison with the Fathers of the Church our present-day theologians are a pathetic group. Most of them lack the elegance, the charm of language, and the style of the Fathers. Content with Aristotle, they treat the mysteries of revelation in the tangled fashion of the logician. Excluding the Platonists from their commentaries, they strangle the beauty of revelation. Yet no less an authority than St. Augustine prefers to express himself in the flowing style that so enhanced the lovely writings of this Platonist school. He prefers them not only because they have so many ideas that are appropriate to our religion but also because the figurative language that they use, abounding in allegories, very closely approaches the language of Scripture itself. The great Christian writers of the past were able to treat even the most arid subjects with a beautiful prose. They enriched and colored their sermons and commentaries with the constant use of allegory. Almost all of them were at home with the writings of Plato and the poets, and they used this literary training to the very best advantage in interpreting the words of Scripture.

It is for this reason that I would recommend that you familiarize yourself with the Fathers. They will lead you to an inner penetration of the word of God, to an understanding of the spiritual worth it contains. This is certainly to be preferred to the scholastic method that invariably ends up in useless disputation. In getting closer to the inner spiritual meaning you will find what is really most important — a hope for the unknown. We have already referred to the Old Testament as abounding in this sort of figurative writing. It is also to be found in the Gospel. For the New Testament has its flesh and its spirit. Paul tells us that we see not the thing itself, but that we see in an obscure manner. We see as through a mirror. We see but an image or a representation of the real object. Christ Himself tells us: "The flesh profits nothing; it is the spirit that gives life." He actually goes beyond what I am saying. As Truth Itself He says that the flesh profits nothing. St. Paul reiterates the same point when he says that the flesh is actually fatal if it does not lead to the spirit. We have already explained that the body cannot even exist without the spirit. Yet the spirit is completely independent of the body.

If then, the spirit is that alone which gives life, then it is obvious enough that our every action should tend toward the spirit. St. Paul, time and time again in his Epistles, exhorts us not to place our trust in the flesh but in the spirit. Here alone is life, liberty, adoption. Everywhere he belittles and condemns the flesh. This is even more evident in the case of our Lord. By giving sight to the blind, by allowing men to eat with unwashed hands, and, on the Sabbath, to lift the ass from the pit and to pick grain from the fields. He shows His disdain for the flesh. The parable of the Pharisee and the Publican, the boastings of the Jews, the bringing of gifts to the altar, are all examples of His condemning the flesh of the law and the superstition of those who preferred to be Jews in public rather than in their secret selves.

He makes this very plain in the case of the Samaritan woman: "Woman, believe me, the hour is coming, when you shall neither on this mountain nor in Jerusalem adore the Father. But the hour is coming, and now is, when the true adorer shall adore the Father in spirit and truth. For the Father also seeks the spiritual to adore Him. God is spirit; and they that adore Him must adore Him in spirit and truth." He meant the same thing when at the marriage feast He turned the water of the cold and insipid letter into the wine of the spirit. And just in case you feel that this was the limit of His disdain for those who seek the flesh and not the spirit, recall to mind what contempt He had for those who eat His flesh and drink His blood in other than a spiritual manner. To whom do you suppose He directed those words? It was certainly to none other than those who think their salvation consists in wearing a blessed medal, or carrying an indulgenced relic. If receiving the very sacrament of His Body is nothing unless done in a spiritual manner, then I think it is plain enough that all other material things are useless unless they are spiritualized.

Perhaps you celebrate Mass daily. Yet if you live as if this were only for your own welfare, and have no concern for the difficulties and needs of your neighbor, you are still in the flesh of the sacrament. The sacrifice of the Mass in this spiritual sense really means that we are of one body with the Body of Christ, we are living members of the Church. If you love nothing except in Christ, if you hold that all of your possessions are the common property of all men, if you make the difficulties and privations of your neighbor your very own, then you may say Mass with great fruit because you do so in a spiritual manner. I think there are far too many who count up how many times they attend Mass and rely almost entirely upon this for their salvation. They are convinced that they owe nothing further to Christ. Leaving Church, they immediately turn to their former habits. I certainly do not hesitate to praise them for getting to Mass but I am forced to condemn them for stopping at this point. They have failed to let what takes place at Mass also take place in their hearts; the death of our Head that is there represented does not take place in their souls. Examine yourself and see if attendance at divine services renders you dead to the world. If you are filled with ambition and envy, even though you offer the sacrifice yourself, you are far from the real significance of the Mass. Christ was slain for you. Sacrifice yourself, then, to Him who sacrificed Himself to the Father. If you believe in what takes place at the altar but fail to enter into the spiritual meaning of it, God will despise your flabby display of religion.

Let us consider a moment the matter of Baptism. Do you really think that the ceremony of itself makes you a Christian? If your mind is preoccupied with the affairs of the world, you may be a Christian on the surface, but inwardly you are a Gentile of the Gentiles. Why is this? It is simply because you have grasped the body of the sacrament, not the spirit. The ceremony consists of washing the body with water, but for you this is not a cleansing of the soul. Salt is placed upon your tongue but your mind remains uncured. The body is anointed with oil but the soul remains unanointed. You have been sprinkled with holy water but this accomplishes nothing unless you cleanse the inner filth of your mind.

Perhaps you are wont to venerate the relics of the saints, yet at the same time you condemn their greatest legacy, the example of their lives. No veneration of Mary is more beautiful than the imitation of her humility. No devotion to the saints is more acceptable to God than the imitation of their virtues. Say you have a great devotion to St. Peter and St. Paul. Then by all means imitate the faith of the former and the charity of the latter. This will certainly be more rewarding than a dozen trips to Rome. Do you really want to honor St. Francis? Then why not give away your wealth to the poor, restrain your evil inclinations, and see in everyone you meet the image of Christ? By avoiding contentions and overcoming evil with good, you will shine forth brighter in the sight of God than a hundred lighted candles. Do you value being buried in the Franciscan habit? The cowl of St. Francis will not benefit you after death if, during your life, you did not imitate his personal integrity. I have continually emphasized that the only complete example of perfect piety is to be found in the imitation of Christ. Yet I do not condemn the imitation of His saints; emulate them in such a way that each of them prompts you to eradicate one or another vice, and practice their particular virtues.

You may have a great veneration for the remains of St. Paul.

If your religion conforms to this then I cannot say that there is really anything wrong with it. But if you merely venerate the ashes of his remains and fail to imitate the resplendent image of him portrayed in his writings, you make your religion a ridiculous thing. You worship his bones hidden away and preserved in nooks and niches, but you fail to worship the great mind of Paul hidden in the Scriptures. A little fragment of his body seen through a glass covering evokes your admiration; why not marvel at his wonderful personality? The ashes you venerate are the very thing that vice will lead to. Let them evoke a feeling of sorrow. Our bodies will all one day be reduced to ashes. When you venerate the image of Christ in the paintings and other works of art that portray Him, think how much more you ought to revere that portrait of His mind that the inspiration of the Holy Spirit has placed in Holy Writ. No artist could possibly have reproduced those words and prayers of Christ that represent Him so exactly in the Gospel. If our Father in heaven finds His perfect reflection in His divine Son, so the words of His Son are the closest image of His divine personality. No relic of our Blessed Lord can possibly approach the strength and beauty of His very self. You may gaze in silent amazement at the tunic that reputedly belonged to Christ, yet you read the wonderful sayings of that same Christ half asleep. You are convinced that it is advantageous to have a small particle of the true Cross in your home, yet this is nothing compared with carrying the mystery of the Cross fixed in your mind. If these external things were the true source of holiness, then certainly there could never have been any people more religious than the Jews. They lived with Him, listened to His words, touched Him — yet most of them rejected Him. What could be more envied than what Judas did, to press the divine mouth with his own? Even our Blessed Lady would not have been the great beneficiary of what Christ did unless she had conceived Him in the Spirit.

Let us carry this idea a bit further. The Apostles are a fine example of this failure of spirit. Even after all the miracles of

Christ, after having listened to His teachings for so many years, after so many proofs of His resurrection, what does He say to them? As He is about to leave them He reproves them for their unbelief. Why was this? Surely it was because the flesh of Christ stood in their way. He tells them: "If I go not, the Paraclete will not come to you; it is necessary that I go." If the very physical presence of Christ is useless to salvation, how can you put your trust in corporeal things? St. Paul actually saw Christ in the flesh. Yet he says: "And if we have known Christ according to the flesh, now we know Him no longer." He meant by this that, in the spirit, he had advanced beyond this kind of knowledge.

Perhaps I am arguing with more verbosity than He who taught the rules. I have a reason for doing so. The attitudes I am talking about are, in my opinion, the worst plague of Christianity. This false set of values brings more ruin than any other, because in appearance it is very close to godliness. There are no vices that are more dangerous than those which have the veneer of virtue. And it is precisely because of this fact that so many good people easily fall into this deception and that the uneducated faithful are led astray. Violent objections are made to anyone who attempts to point out these things. I care very little about objections to my criticisms so long as they have been approved by ecclesiastical authority. They are signs, supports of piety. And they are quite necessary for children in Christ, at least until they have become a little more mature. Even those more advanced in perfection should not scorn them, lest their scorn work great harm among the simple and uninstructed. My approval rests on the assumption that they are steps, or gradations, that lead to more appropriate means of salvation.

But to place the whole of religion in external ceremonies is sublime stupidity. This amounts to revolt against the spirit of the Gospel and is a reversion to the superstitions of Judaism. St. Paul was incessant in his attempt to remove the Jews from their faith in external works. I feel that the vast majority of

Christians have sunk once again into this unhealthy situation.

Why do I say the majority? Because I think that even the casual observer will admit that not only the priests and theologians but also their flocks have been infested with this error. The salt is unsalted. It shames me to mention how many of them observe these foolish man-made ceremonies; the way in which such ceremonies are relentlessly imposed upon others as the only way of salvation is appalling. And they are hopelessly convinced that there is no other way than the one they have invented. They have become so imbued with self-righteousness that they fancy themselves St. Pauls and St. Anthonys. Thinking themselves great authorities, they impose their narrow way of life on others as if it were a divine mandate. Look at most of them who have grown old in this way of life. If there is any resemblance to Christ in them, it remains hidden. They are so filled with reeking vices, so introspective and morose, that they can hardly live with themselves, let alone with others. They are grown cold in charity, persistent in hatred; their speech is poisonous, and their jealousies unbridled. They are even lacking in those virtues which the pagans of old possessed. Their many years of labor end in a suspicion of others and contentiousness that surpasses the heathen's. If they had walked in the spirit and not in the flesh, then where are the fruits of the spirit? Where is their charity? Where is their peace toward all men? Where long-suffering, modesty, and chastity? Where, in short, is the image of Christ in their behavior?

Of course they will tell you with great pride that they do not consort with prostitutes, that they are not thieves, or desecrators of holy things. They will boast that they have kept their vows. Yet is not this exactly what the Pharisee said? "I am not like other men, extortioners, adulterers. I fast twice a week." I would much prefer to have a Publican confessing his sins than this kind of Pharisee rehearsing his good deeds. Because you have taken the vows of religion, does this excuse you from performing those things that you promised long ago when you were baptised?

Surely these people are transgressing God's commandments because of certain foolish, man-made traditions. Or am I wrong in contending that Christianity is a spiritual life? Listen again to St. Paul, speaking to the Romans:

> There is therefore no condemnation to them who are in Christ Jesus, who walk not according to the flesh. For the law of the spirit of life in Christ Jesus has delivered me from the law of sin and death. For what the law could not do because it was weak through the flesh, God, in sending His own Son in the likeness of sinful flesh, condemned as sin the flesh, that the justification of the law might be fulfilled in us who walk not according to the flesh, but according to the spirit. For they who are according to the flesh relish the things that are of the flesh; but they who are of the spirit mind the things that are of the spirit. For the wisdom of the flesh is death; but the wisdom of the spirit is life and peace. Because the wisdom of the flesh is an enemy to God, for it is not subject to the law of God and neither can it ever be. And they who are in the flesh cannot please God.

How could this possibly be said in a more apt manner and with greater emphasis?

Now most of these people we are describing are not in the least affected by these words. Deceived by their own pleasures, they think that when St. Paul talks about the "flesh" he is referring only to adulterers and fornicators. The expression "wisdom of the flesh" they twist to mean the study of secular literature (as they call it). And in both respects they find real reason to applaud themselves. For in fact they are not adulterers and they are outrageously unlearned in all letters. On the other hand, life in the spirit they fancy to require nothing else than what they themselves are doing. If these folk had observed Paul's language as diligently as they forcibly condemn Cicero's, they would certainly have known only too well that the apostle calls "flesh" that which is visible, "spirit" that which is invisible. Indeed, he teaches that visible things ought everywhere to serve invisible, not the opposite. Preposterously they accommodate Christ to these things which really ought to be adapted to Him.

If you want sufficient proof that the word of the flesh does not pertain so much to lust or lechery, listen to what the same Apostle, acting as is his wont, writes to the Colossians: "No one can put you in the wrong by persistent and studied humility and the worship of angels, being absorbed in the visions he has seen and groundlessly conceited over his mere human mind. Such people loose their connection with the head, from which the whole body through its ligaments and sinews must be governed and united if it is to grow in the divine way." And lest you doubt that he speaks of those who, relying on certain bodily ceremonies, cry out against the spiritual zeal of others, listen to what follows: "Therefore if you be risen with Christ, seek the things which are above where Christ sits at the right hand of the Father; be wise in the things of heaven, not in the things of the earth." Then, in teaching the precepts of the spiritual life, he gives a warning — a warning in which he mentions nothing of ceremonies, clothing, food, or prayer — a warning in which he reiterates all that he has already said: "Mortify yourselves: he who is a slave to fornication, uncleanness, lust, evil desires and avarice is a slave to sin." Not satisfied with this admonition, he continues: "Cast off all anger, indignation, malice: strip off the old man and put on the new man who has been reborn in the knowledge of God."

I do not deny that you practice such observances as vigils, fastings, silence, and prayer. But these things notwithstanding, unless I see the fruits of the spirit, I shall not believe that you are in the spirit. You have not yet conquered the works of the flesh, and I have but to name the sins common among you — anger, quarreling, cursing, backbiting, pride, lack of faith, vanity, deceit, flattery . . . to give proof of what I say. If Paul were here now what conclusions could he draw from your actions?

You believe that because you are faithful in matters which are venial you have the right to break the law in matters which are grave. Those men who do evil because of the hope of a great reward are not more wicked than you who break the law and have no hope of such a reward. In fact, a light cause does not excuse guilt but increases it. Of what value are long hours of prayer if you lack a proper intention? You would do well to remember that the more quickly a man will sin, the more wicked he is.

I am not speaking of those monks whose evil ways are known by all; rather I speak of those who are looked upon as angels by the people, and I trust that in referring to such hypocrites, no good men will be offended or be included in the number of those whom I criticize. If they are good men, let them rejoice that they are forewarned concerning those things which pertain to salvation. Though there are many men who have made themselves well acquainted with the holy mysteries, even in this group there are a large number who minimize what should be emphasized. Anyone who cares to investigate this matter of which I speak will find very few monks who do not walk in the flesh. It is because they are yet infants that this is so, and as long as they remain in their infancy, they will be as oxen under the yoke, neither aspiring to liberty of spirit nor attaining the fullness of charity.

Paul cries out to the Galatians: "Stand and never again be confined by the yoke of slavery. The law was our tutor, bringing us to Christ, to find in faith our justification. When faith comes, we are no longer under the rule of a tutor; through faith in Jesus Christ, we are now God's sons. In those childhood days of ours we toiled away at the schoolroom tasks which were given us until the appointed time came. Then God sent His Son on a mission to us. He was born of a woman and became a subject of the law in order to ransom those who were subject to the law and to make them sons by adoption. To prove that we are sons, God has sent the Spirit of His Son into our hearts crying out in us, Abba, Father. No longer, then, are we slaves; we are now sons." In the same vein, Paul concludes: "You, brethren, have been called to freedom. Do not permit this freedom to give corrupt nature a foothold; you must be servants still, but now you serve one another in a spirit of charity. After all, the whole of the law is summed up in one phrase: you shall love your neighbor as yourself. If you continually annoy each other, it is to be feared that you will wear each other out."

In his Epistle to the Romans, Paul declared that: "You have received the Spirit of adoption of sons of God whereby you cry, Abba, Father." The same Apostle, in his letter to Timothy, mentions that we should exercise ourselves in piety, for piety is profitable to us. In speaking to the Corinthians he writes: "God is Spirit; where the Spirit is, there is liberty."

The words of St. Paul should leave us with the lesson that it is the Spirit who is the author of love and liberty. Where the Spirit is, these two qualities must also be. We do not have to go to Paul to learn this lesson — we need go no further than Christ Himself. Love was, above all else, the message that He came to teach. To the Ten Commandments of the Old Law, He saw fit to add one other — "A new commandment I give unto you, that you love one another." It is not to be wondered at, then, that Paul emphasizes love, and it is not surprising that in his Epistle to the Corinthians he places love above miracles, prophesying, and speaking with the tongues of angels.

Charity does not consist in many visits to churches, in many prostrations before the statues of saints, in the lighting of candles, or in the repetition of a number of designated prayers. Of all these things God has no need. Paul declares charity to be the edification of one's neighbor, the attempt to integrate all men into one body so that all men may become one in Christ, the loving of one's neighbor as one's self. Charity for Paul has many facets; he is charitable who rebukes the erring, who teaches the ignorant, who lifts up the fallen, who consoles the down-hearted, who supports the needy. If a man is truly charitable he will devote, if needs be, all his wealth, all his zeal, and all his care to the benefit of others.

Just as Christ gave Himself completely for us, so also should we give ourselves for our neighbor. If the attitude of the religious were comparable to the attitude of Christ, the life of the religious would be much easier and much happier than we now know it to be. No longer would the religious be sad, weary, superstitious, and prone to many temptations; no longer would he fall a victim to the vices of the laity. You who are religious claim to be followers of the rule of Augustine; were he now to return to this life, I wonder if he would recognize as disciples you who turn not to the rule of the Apostles as Augustine desired, but to the superstitions of the Jews. Some among you attempt to justify the emphasis you place on little things by claiming that unless you are faithful in the less important matters, you are opening the door to greater vices. This view deserves some commendation, but there is also a danger that, in emphasizing the less, you may forget the more.

In short, you must avoid the horns of the dilemma. To observe these unimportant things is, of course, wholesome, but to make them the whole object of your devotion is extremely dangerous. St. Paul recommends ceremonies but he does not bind us to the law, since we are free in Christ. He is not opposed to good works (without them it would be impossible to be a good Christian), yet they do not make the Christian. Paul does not put great worth in the works of Abraham; why should you trust so in your works? Did not God chide the Jews of old for their empty sacrifices and fasts? He tells us that not every man who says "Lord, Lord" is saved and points out that the practice of charity is more important than empty ceremonies. Help him who is oppressed, aid the fatherless, the motherless, the friendless, defend the widow. He recommends that, instead of fasting, we cancel the debt of him who owes us, that we lighten the burden of him who labors, that we share our bread with the hungry, that we house the homeless and clothe the naked.

I am not advocating that you neglect the mandates of the Church or that you despise honorable traditions and godly customs. If, however, you consider yourselves to be good religious striving for perfection, let your acts be those of one who sincerely desires perfection. If there is a question as to what works should come first, there should be no doubt in your minds. I am not condemning manual works, but I am trying to impress upon you that such works are of little value unless they are accompanied by internal piety. God is a Spirit and is appeased by spiritual sacrifices. A minor poet once wrote: "If God is mind, in poems he's revealed; with a pure mind, then, you ought to worship him." Each one of us should meditate upon these words. While it is true that the author is a pagan and that he has no place of prominence in the world of letters, yet his message, which is read by few and understood by fewer, should not be despised. His advice is worthy of a great theologian. God is mind, the most pure and most simple mind of all; therefore, he must be worshipped with a pure mind.

You believe God to be greatly touched by such material things as a slain bull or the smell of incense; you think that burned wax is a sacrifice. Why, then, did David say: "An afflicted spirit is a sacrifice to God"? If God despised the blood of goats and bulls, he will not despise a contrite and humble heart. If you attend fervently to these things which men expect you to do, spend much more time on those things which God expects of you. Of what advantage to you is a body covered by a religious habit if that same body possesses a mind that is worldly? If your habit is white, should not your mind be white, too? If your tongue is at rest in public, should not your mind be also at rest? What does it profit you when you kneel to pray if your mind is not in accord with the mind of God? You venerate the wood of the Cross and forget the mystery of the Cross. You fast and abstain from those things which do not pollute men, yet you do not refrain from obscene conversations, which are a cause of pollution not only to yourself but also to those to whom you speak.

Why do you feed the body and starve the soul? You keep the Sabbath outwardly, but in the secret recesses of your mind you permit all kinds of vices to run rampant. Your body does not commit adultery, but you make your soul to be an adulterer by your greediness. You sing psalms, but your thoughts do not keep pace with your tongue. You bless with the mouth and curse with the heart. You hear the word of God spoken to you, but you refuse it entrance to your heart. Listen closely to the words of the prophet: "Unless you hear within, your soul will weep." And again, "You hear but you do not understand." Blessed are they who hear the word of God internally. Happy are they to whom the Lord speaks inwardly, for their salvation is assured. Do you wonder why the daughter of the king, she who was goodness itself, was ordered by David to listen within for the voice of God?

Finally, what does it mean if you do not do the evil things which your mind lusts after? What does it mean if you perform good deeds in public, but allow evil deeds to dominate your mind? Where is the profit if you have the appearance of a Jerusalem, but the character of a Sodom, an Egypt, or a Babylon? If it is to a man's credit that his body walks in Christ's footsteps, it is more to his credit that his mind has followed the way of Christ. If it is a wonderful thing to have touched the Lord's sepulcher, it is more wonderful to have learned the lesson of the mystery of the sepulcher. You who reproach yourselves when you confess your sins to a priest, how will you feel when God accuses you of the same sins? Perhaps you believe that by wax seals, by sums of money, or by pilgrimages, your sins are washed away immediately. If you are confident that these are the ways of forgiveness, you are sadly mistaken. If you wish to be forgiven, you, who have loved what you should have hated and who have hated what you should have loved, must attack the enemy within.

Perhaps I am devoting too much time to discussing your external actions, but I will not be convinced of your sanctity until you begin to hate and to flee those things which you used to love. Mary Magdalene loved much, and many sins were forgiven her. The more you love Christ the more you will hate your vices, for just as the shadow follows the body, the hatred of sin follows the love of godliness. I would prefer that you really hate your evil deeds internally rather than enumerate them ten times before a priest.

Therefore, my brethren, put on Christ. Take as your rule that you no longer wish to crawl upon the ground, with the beasts, but to rise upon those wings which sprout in the minds of those who love. Advance from the body to the spirit, from the visible world to the invisible, from things sensible to things intelligible, from things compound to things simple. If you come near to the Lord, He will come near to you; if you make a sincere effort to escape from the chains of blindness with which the love of sensible things has bound you, He will come to you, and you, no longer chained to the things of earth, will be enveloped in the silence of God.

### Sixth Rule.

From among the many thoughts which have entered my mind since I began this letter to you, I think it would be fitting to choose a sixth rule — a rule which, incidentally, is observed by too few of those who claim to be followers of Christ. If we would be holy, we must go to the sole archetype of godliness, Christ Himself. Anyone who refuses to do this is outside the pale. Plato in his *Republic* points out that no man can defend virtue unless he has trained his mind in opinions regarding the true nature of good and evil. We can see then how dangerous it is if false opinions of those things that pertain to well-being should sink deeply into the mind.

A man's actions are mere expressions of his inner convictions; for a man to live as to always act well, he must be taught even from infancy the things that are of Christ. Since nothing takes root more deeply in a man's mind than that which is taught to him in his earliest years, children should always be protected from any vestige of evil example. A child, being what he is, is most susceptible to example; therefore let good example be given always, so that no sinful errors may creep into the child's mind and so that salutary habits may take firm root. He who has such salutary habits will follow virtue of his own accord, and he will judge those who do wrong to be deserving of pity, and not of imitation. Socrates might be mentioned here, as he points out that virtue is nothing other than the knowledge of things that are to be sought after or of things that are to be avoided, with a distinction made between knowledge of goodness and a love of it. Vice, then, can proceed from no other source than wrong opinions. Both he who loves Christ and follows Him, and he who loves evil pleasures, think that they seek something that is good for themselves. The world has never advanced in goodness to the point where common opinion does not still give its approval to what is basically evil.

Today as ever in the past there are many men who are mere imitators of the crowd; if such men see someone of importance bring forth a new opinion or perform some action, they must adopt that opinion or imitate the action. Their norm is not the morality of the deed performed, but the prominence of the one who performs the deed. They seem to think that all acts of a person in the public eye must of necessity be virtuous. But what is done is virtuous only if it squares with the rule of Christ. Indeed, a man ought to be suspicious of anything that pleases the majority, for the number of those whose hearts are possessed by Christian simplicity, poverty, and truth will always be small.

Small as this group may be, however, to it alone belongs the kingdom of heaven. The way of virtue is narrow and it is trodden by few, but no other leads to life. Anyone who intends to build well must seek his exemplar not from that which is most popular, but from that which is most perfect. When a painter wants a model, for example, he chooses only the best painting. Our exemplar is Christ, and He alone we should imitate; it is permitted, too, of course, that we seek to emulate those models of virtue who have patterned their lives on the life of Christ.

Faith without morals worthy of faith only serves to assure men of damnation. Christians today seem to be lacking in their respect for the moral law, and, to be truthful, there have been pagans whose moral code was on a higher plane than the present moral law of many Christians. If you find what I say unworthy of belief, unroll the ancient records and compare the moral law of the pagans with the customs of today. When in the past was true honesty thought more contemptible than it is now? When were riches, however acquired, held in higher esteem? When was luxury more unfettered? When were fornication and adultery less shameless and less punished? Today, even the princes condone vices, and a fashionable appearance covers a multitude of sins. The only disgrace and the greatest evil is poverty. In times past, in the games of the pagans, it was customary to fling defamatory taunts at fornicators, filthy persons, the boastful, and those who made of money a god; the pagan crowd recognized some merit in one who would disguise his vices. Today these same vices are applauded even by Christian leaders. Looking again to the past, the audiences of the Athenian theatre did not tolerate the actor in a certain play by Euripides who played the role of a man who preferred money to all the other goods of human life. They hissed the actor so lustily that the author was forced to entreat them to be patient, and to wait for the outcome of the play, so that the fate of the man entranced by greed might be seen. The audience would not listen to the plea of the author, and the play came to an abrupt end.

This is just one example of how a part of the world felt toward vice; there were many men of integrity to be found, men who preferred faith to money, virtue to life, a right conscience to honors or wealth. I do not have to remind you of the sanctity of Photion, of the poverty of Fabritius, of the generosity of Camillus, of the asceticism of Brutus, of the modesty of Pythagoras, of the unassailable continence of Socrates, of the integrity of Cato, and of the example of a thousand other men. The books of pagan antiquity are illumined by the description of their virtues. Is it not to the eternal shame of all Christians that men who were pagans should be so worthy of our admiration? Augustine testifies in his *Confessions* that he should have been converted to Christ much sooner, for even as one not belonging to the Church of Christ he held money in contempt, had no use for honors, was not moved by glory, and denied full play to pleasure to the extent that, as a young man, he was content with one mistress, to whom he preserved conjugal fidelity.

Today it would be a difficult task to find examples such as I have gathered from the pagan world even among the nobility, the ecclesiastics, and the monks of Christendom. If a virtuous person be found, he is pointed out and laughed at. By some he is called a dull-witted hypocrite, ignorant and insane; by others he is judged not even to be a man. What kind of veneration for the teaching of Christ is this, when we hold nothing to be more senseless, more debased, and more shameful than to devote oneself sincerely and wholeheartedly to the service of Christ? If the opinion of the mass of Christians is any criterion, then we must judge Christ's life to have been in vain, and we must conclude that His teaching does not apply equally to all, and that Christianity is now a different religion than it once was. From what I have said, then, learn these lessons: resist evil with your whole mind, and measure the value of a thing by its worth in the eyes of Christ.

Do not be moved by those men, many of them prudent, who think that they have a claim to fame because of the prominence of their forebears. Be amused at such men who seek to base their reputation on the reputation of others, and realize that the only true nobility consists in being reborn in Christ, in being engrafted into His body, in being made one with God. If those who claim to be nobles desire to live in the halls of princes, that is their affair; your business is to be "a humble person in the house of God." Do not neglect the infirm and the foolish — the ignoble in the eyes of the world. In Adam all of us are born ignoble; true nobility means to be a servant of Christ. Recall to mind what Christ said to the Jews when they boasted of their descent from Abraham: "You are of your father, the devil; and the works of your father you will do." Paul, in judging nobility, was of the same mind as Christ: "Not all who are of Israel by circumcision are Israelites nor are all who are of the seed of Abraham his children."

To be truly ignoble is to serve wickedness, and one who is a slave to evil does not know Christ, for Christ knows only those who do the will of His Father who is in heaven. Unless Christ has lied, he who does the devil's work has the devil for his father; but Christ could not lie. He is of the highest nobility who is a son and heir to God, a brother and coheir of Christ. The coat of arms of this family is the Cross, which should be the insignia of all Christians, along with the crown of thorns, the keys, the lance, the wounds of the Lord, which Paul gloried to bear in his body. How true it is that the common people often think him blessed and happy who has accumulated vast wealth. Yet you ought to consider him as being blessed who has as his chief possession Christ Himself. Consider him as truly happy who has bought the pearl of great price — purity of mind — at the cost of his wealth or even his health. The wealth that the common people envy is the very weed which chokes out the seed of the word of God.

Do not consider yourself a whit better if you surpass either Midas or Croesus in wealth, but rather more bound, more impeded, more burdened. Actually he has enough who can despise such things. He to whom Christ has promised that nothing will be lacking, has enough to look forward to. He will not hunger who wisely savors the manna of the divine word. He will not go naked who puts on Christ. Consider this alone a loss: the many times one has departed from piety and has increased in vices. Consider it a great gain, when the mind by an increase of virtue has been improved. Consider that you lack nothing if you possess Him in whom are all things.

What is this that the miserable call pleasure? It is utter insanity, and plainly (as the Greeks used to say) the laughter of Ajax, sweet poison, smooth ruin. True pleasure is the joy of a pure conscience. The most delicious banquets are the study of the Holy Scriptures. The most pleasing songs are the psalms of the Holy Spirit. The most joyous fellowship is the communion of saints. The highest delights are in the enjoyment of truth. Only purify your eyes, your ears, your palate, and Christ will begin to become sweet to you. When He has truly been tasted, all pleasures, all delights, in comparison with Christ will seem as vomit. That is not really sweet which tastes so to anyone, but which tastes sweet to a healthy man. If to a fevered man water tastes like wine, no one calls that pleasure, but disease. You are mistaken if you do not believe tears to be far more joyful to pious men than laughter, jeers, and pranks to the impious; fasting is sweeter to the former than cocks, pheasants, partridges, or sturgeon to the latter; the frugal little meals of the former, furnished with their cabbages and Pythagorean beans, are far more elegant than the sumptuous delicacies of the latter.

True pleasure consists in this, that out of love of Christ, we are never moved by false pleasures. Take for example how the world abuses the expressions love and hate. When a foolish young man is completely out of his mind for the affection of a common wench, the common folk call this love. There is in fact no truer form of hate. True love looks primarily to the benefit of another. Whoever seeks after his own pleasure does not really love the object of his affections but rather himself. No man can hate except he first hate himself. Nonetheless there are occasions when to truly love is to hate well, and to hate well is to love well. In the case of a young man about to seduce a girl with flattery and gifts, is this love or hate? What is more hateful than the action of those parents who, neglecting to discipline their children, pamper them to the point that they inculcate false values that will be detrimental to their eternal welfare? If you kill the sinner you save the man. If you destroy what man has made you will restore what God has fashioned.

Take, for example, power and weakness, courage and cowardice: what does popular error think them to be? Do they not call him powerful who can easily harm whomever he will? Although to be able to do harm, to inflict evil, is a power excessively hateful, it is common to cowardice, along with flies and scorpions, and the devil himself.

God alone is truly powerful, who could neither do harm if He wished nor want to do it if He could, for His very nature is to do good. But how, then, does this powerful One harm man? Will He snatch money away, will He strike the body, will He take away life? If He does this to a pious man, He has given good for evil-doing; if He does it to a wicked man, He has but furnished the occasion, the man has harmed himself. For no one is harmed except by himself. No one prepares to harm another unless he has already far more gravely harmed himself. You prepare to cause me a loss of money, but since you have already lost charity, you have suffered the gravest loss of all. You cannot inflict a wound upon me unless you have already received at your own hands a much more frightful hurt. You will not deprive men of the body, unless you have already safely slain your own soul. Yet does not Paul boast that he can do all things in Christ, for he is feeble in inflicting injury but exceedingly strong in bearing it? The crowd considers him strong and courageous who is fierce and of weak mind, who boils over with anger at any injury however slight, who returns reproach for reproach, evil deed for evil deed. On the other hand they call him who disregards or conceals an injury which he has sustained, cowardly, pusillanimous, spiritless. What is more foreign to greatness of mind than to be driven by a mere word from peace of mind; hence not to be able to condemn folly as alien, so that you do not think yourself to be a man unless you heap curse upon curse? Yet how much more manly, with full and lofty purpose, is it to be able to ignore an injury, and besides that to return good for evil.

I would not call him a brave man who would attack his enemy or storm his fortress without regard for his own life. Rather, call brave whoever overcomes his mind, or whoever wills good to those who harm him.

Let us also examine that which the world calls glory, ignominy, and shame. You are praised. Why, and by whom? If on account of wickedness by wicked folk, this indeed is false glory and ignominy. You are abused, mocked. For what reason, and by whom? If on account of piety and innocence, by evil folk, this is not ignominy, for there is no truer glory. Remain calm, even if the whole world hisses and hoots at you. What Christ approves cannot but be glorious. And if He applaud or acclaim anything by mortals as "well done!" one must be ashamed of what displeases Him.

It is commonly called prudence to anticipate events, to establish firmly what has taken place, and even to look forward into the future. How often is it not heard that so and so is temperate, sagacious, prudent, foresighted, concerning those things which make life more comfortable for a short time? By this is meant the world, which is both false and his father. Yet what does the Truth say? "Fool, this night your soul will be required of you." He had filled the barns with the harvest, he had furnished all the storehouses with provisions, he had laid up in his house very much money. He thought that nothing remained. All he needed to do (so he thought) was to enjoy the produce of his fields. Yet the Gospel calls this foolishness. What indeed is more foolish, more senseless, than to gape at shadows and lose the true things. We laugh at this when we see it in Aesop's dog. And in the morals of Christians ought it not the more to be laughed at, or rather wept over? It is an inexperienced merchant indeed who does not anticipate a shortage of produce or an inflationary season by stocking up his supplies. Yet how foolish it is to take such great care in hoarding for this life, which is but a fleeting shadow. In this world God has promised to take care of all things necessary. He will provide both here and hereafter for all who confide in Him.

Consider another error. They call a person sharp and intelligent who, by relying on rumors and hearsay, knows everything that goes on in the world. What is happening in the world of business, what the king of the English busies himself about, what is new at Rome, what is stirring among the French, how the Dacians and Scythians are getting along, what the princes are deliberating about. In short, they call wise the individual practiced in chatting about all sorts of business, among all kinds of men. What is more unthinking, more ignorant, than to inquire into those things which take place far away and have nothing to do with you, if you do not also ponder over those things which you carry in your breast, and pertain to you alone? You tell me about British troubles; tell me rather what rages in your breast — anger, envy, lust, ambition. To what extent have you brought these vices under your control? What is the hope of victory? How great a part of the war has already been won? How well trained is your reason? In these things I will pronounce you expert, if you have been vigilant, if you have kept ears and eyes equally alert, if you have been wise and circumspect. And that "knowledge" which the world is wont to cast upon us I shall cast back to it. Fruitless is the wisdom of him who has no knowledge of himself.

Toward this end, if you care for all mankind, you will drive out joys, hopes, fears, zeal, purposes. You will find all these full of error. Men call good evil and evil good. They make bitter things sweet and sweet bitter. They make light darkness and darkness light. Indeed, this is by far the greatest disturbance for men. You should at the same time condemn these men, so as not to wish to be like them, and to feel pity, as you want them to become like you. To use Augustine's words, it is sometimes fitting to weep for those deserving of laughter, or to laugh at those deserving of weeping. "Do not be conformed in evil to this world, but be reformed in the newness of your mind, that you may prove, not what men admire, but what is the good, and the acceptable, and the perfect will of God." You are close to danger and plainly beginning to slip, if you begin to look about at what the majority are doing, if you begin to clutch at what they believe. You are the offspring of life and light. "Let the dead bury their dead." "The blind leaders of the blind fall at the same time into the pit." Take care that you do not move the eyes of your heart away from your example, Christ. You will not err if you follow the leadership of the Truth. You will not cast yourself among the shadows while you walk after the light. You will not shudder when the light shines through, if you distinguish the counterfeit good from the true, the true evils from the false. You will not imitate the blindness of the multitude, burning with desire for some Euripus or other with each of the passions in turn — anger, envy, love, hate, hope, fear, joy, pain. Brahmans, Cynics, Stoics fight for their doctrines. When the world loudly contradicts them, when everyone hisses and hoots at them, they pertinaciously urge what they have earlier persuaded themselves to be true. Dare likewise to fix the rules of your own sect deep within. Dare to adopt completely and firmly the views of your maker.

### Opinions Worthy of a Christian.

Let these always stand before you as the paradoxes of true Christianity: that no Christian think himself to have been born for himself, nor wish to live for himself. All that he has, or is, he does not credit to himself; he gives credit to God as Author of all his goods, and considers them to be the common property of all. Christian charity recognizes no property. Let him love the pious in Christ and the impious also for Christ's sake. Even when we were His enemies He so loved us that He gave Himself wholly for our ransom. The pious He embraces because they are good. The impious He embraces equally, that He may render them good. He certainly hates no man, no more than a faithful doctor hates a sick person. Toward vices, however, He is unfriendly. The graver the disease, the greater the care that pure charity will bring to it. A man is an adulterer. He commits sacrilege. He is a Turk. Let the act of adultery be execrated, not the man. Let the sacrilege, not the man, be despised. Let the Turk be killed, not the man. Let him put forth effort that the impious man he has made of himself may perish. But let him also wish that the man whom God has made may be saved. Let him sincerely desire well of all men; let him pray well, let him do good. Nor let him harm the deserving, and benefit the undeserving. Let him manifest as much joy over the good fortunes of all men as he does over his own. Let him be grieved over the ill fortunes of all men, not differently than he is over his own. Doubtless this it is that the Apostles urged, to weep with those who weep, to rejoice with those who rejoice.

Let him, even, feel another's evil more heavily than he does his own. Let him be happier about his brother's good fortune than his own. It is not the Christian's way to reason thus: "What have I to do with him? I know not whether he be white or black, he is unknown, he is a stranger, he never deserved anything well of me. He has even at times harmed me." At least remember that Christ gave none of His gifts to you because of your merit. He wanted His benefits to be reciprocated, not to Himself, but to your neighbor. See what your neighbor lacks, and what you can do for him. Consider this: He is your brother in the Lord, coheir with you in Christ, a member of the same body, redeemed by the same blood, a comrade in the common faith, called to the same grace and happiness in the future life. It is just as the Apostle says: "One body, and one spirit, as you are called in one hope of your vocation. One Lord, one faith, one baptism, One God and Father of us all, who is above all, and through all, and in us all." How, then, can you consider a stranger he who is joined to you with so many intimate bonds of unity? Among the pagans these considerations are of great weight: that a person be a citizen of the same city, or that he be an ally, a cousin, a familiar friend, a friend of the family, a rich person, a member of the nobility. In Christ all things are either nothing or they are, as St. Paul says, all united in One. Bear in mind that we are all, always and everywhere, one flesh in Christ. Whatever happens to one member of the body happens to the entire body. We are all members of one another. The head of the body is Jesus Christ, the head of Christ is God. Whatever happens to you happens to Christ, to God. All are one — God, Christ, the body and the members. Diversity is the mother of hate.

No man is a Christian just because he is a noble rather than a member of a town mob, a rustic instead of a city dweller, a patrician instead of a plebian, a magistrate instead of a private citizen, a rich man instead of a pauper, a famous man rather than an obscure one, a strong man rather than a weak, an Italian rather than a German, a Frenchman instead of a Briton, a

Briton instead of a Scot, a grammarian instead of a cleric, a physician instead of a man of law, a single individual instead of a married person, a cleric instead of a layman, a priest instead of a monk.

Where is love, which even loves the enemy when the name is changed? A different color of clothing, belt, or shoe, and such trivialities of men, can make me hateful to you. Why not banish all this childish trumpery and whatever else pertains to the matter? Then we can accustom ourselves to hold before our eyes the truth which Paul in many places drives home, that we are all, in Christ as Head, members of one body, animated by the same Spirit. If we live in Him, we will not envy happier members, and will willingly help weaker ones. We will know that we have received a benefit when we help our neighbor, and also know that we have been injured when harm has been done to our brother. Nor should anyone strive for himself alone, but, to the best of his ability, contribute to the common store which he has received of God. Thus all things may flow back whence they flowed forth, namely, to the Head.

This, indeed, is what Paul writes to the Corinthians: "For as the body is one, and has many members, and all the members of the body, whereas they are many, yet are one body; so also is Christ."

And elsewhere he bids all to bear one another's burdens, since we are all members of one another. See, therefore, whether they belong to this body, whom now and again you hear speaking in this way: "My property came to me by inheritance; I do not possess it by fraud. Why should I not enjoy it according to my own inclination, and abuse it? Why should I give anything to them to whom I owe nothing? I squander, I lose it, yet what is lost is mine. It makes no difference to others." Your fellow member opens wide his mouth with fasting, while you reek with the flesh of partridge. Your unclothed brother horrifies you, yet your clothing is rotting with moths and decay. You gamble away a thousand pieces of gold in one night, while some poor girl, in dire need, prostitutes her body and loses her

soul, for which Christ poured out His soul. You say: "What
has that to do with me? My own concerns take up all my
thoughts." Do you see yourself a Christian with this mind, fit
not even for a man? You hear in the crowd the reputation of
such and such a person being injured, yet you remain silent or
perhaps smile at the detractor. "I would," you say, "have stop-
ped what was said, if any of it had pertained to me. Yet I have
nothing in common with him who was harmed." Therefore,
you have nothing in common with the body, if you have nothing
in common with a member of it. Nor is there anything in common with the head, if there is nothing in common with the body.

They say: "It is lawful to repel force with force." I do not
tarry over what the imperial laws permit. I wonder at this —
how those voices penetrated into the ways of Christians. "I
have harmed someone, but I was provoked to it. I preferred
to give evil rather than to receive it." Granted that human
laws do not punish what they have permitted. Yet what is Christ
your leader going to do if you defraud His law, which is given
in Matthew's Gospel? "But I say to you, not to resist evil; but
if any man strike you on your right cheek, turn to him the other
also." You reply: "These words which He has spoken do not
apply to me. He spoke to the Apostles, the perfect." Have you
not heard that you are the sons of your Father? If you do not
desire to be a son of God, the law means nothing to you. Yet
there is no good man, indeed, who does not want to be perfect.
If you do not desire reward, that rule is not enjoined upon you.
There follows: "If you love those who love you, what sort of
recompense will you have?" None to speak of. Nor does virtue
consist in doing this, but it is a crime not to do it. Nothing is
owed to anyone where like repays like. Listen to St. Paul, who
was both a wise man and the best interpreter of Christ's law.
Bless them that persecute you, render to no man evil for evil,
and in so far as it is possible be at peace with all men. Do not
give way to anger for it is written, vengeance is mine. But if
your enemy is hungry give him to eat, if he be thirsty give him
to drink. In so doing you will heap coals of fire on his head,

that is to say, you will enkindle the flame of love in him. Be not overcome by evil but overcome evil with goodness.

You ask yourself, what will happen if my kindness allows others to increase their audacity and if my suffering an old injury produces a new one? If you can avoid evil by suffering it yourself, do so. Try to help your enemy by overcoming him with kindness and meekness. If this does not help, then it is better that one perish than both of you. It is better that you be enriched with the advantage of patience than to render evil for evil. This ought to be a universal rule of Christian men that they try to surpass one another in meekness and good deeds, and that with benevolence they avoid hate, backbiting, and vindictiveness even toward the most repulsive. It is not enough to practice the golden rule in this matter. The greater your position the more ready you ought to be to forgive another's crime. If you are a person of noble birth then this attitude of mind will only enhance your nobility. If you are a gifted person then try the more earnestly to forgive the ignorance of the unlearned. The greater your gifts, the greater the debt to your brother. If you should be wealthy bear ever in mind that you are the dispenser, not the master, of your riches.

You believed that only to monks was property forbidden and poverty imposed? You have erred, for it pertains to all Christians. The civil law punishes you if you take to yourself what belongs to another. It does not punish you if you refuse your possessions to a needy brother. Yet even so Christ will punish you. If you should be a ruler do not allow your position to make you more arrogant, but rather more concerned with the care of your subjects. You might say, I am not an official of the Church, neither a pastor nor a bishop. Granted you are not, you are nevertheless a Christian man, and a member of the Church. Too many today hold Christ in such contempt that they think it is an excellent thing to have absolutely nothing to do with Him, and despise their neighbors to the extent that they are associated with Him. How often do we not hear from the laity the terrible accusations they hurl against the clergy and the monks, accusations of incest and sacrilege. It amazes me that they do not also object to those who are baptized and treat the Christian name as the Saracens do. If they condemn an unworthy priest, an unworthy cleric, an irreligious monk, let them distinguish the person from his calling. Whoever takes pride in the number of virgins he has deflowered, or the spoils of war he has looted, or the money he has won at gambling, should, it seems to me, have little grounds for laying accusations at the feet of the monks and the clergy. He should rather be ashamed of his own life.

It is easy enough to see what these nominal Christians think of Christ. There is not one Master for the bishops and another for the civic officials. Both must one day render an account to the same judge. If you, as a leader, look to any other source than Him, it matters little in receiving and administering your office whether the world accuse you of simony; He will in the end punish you. If you work to obtain an office in government only to increase your own profit, to the detriment of the common good, or to avenge some grudge, then your office is nothing other than bribery and theft before God. If you are a civil magistrate who delights in tracking down criminals only to feather your own nest with their stolen goods, then what difference is there between them and yourself, except that they steal from citizens and you steal from them.

I might add in conclusion that unless you are prepared to exercise your office in the defense of what is just, even to the loss of your life, Christ will not approve of your administration. Plato tells us that no man is worthy of an office who takes great joy in it. If you are a prince take care lest you be seduced by flattery. If you are a legislator remember that the laws you enact bind you as well as others. If you think that the exhortations of the clergy to the common people do not pertain to you, then do not forget that there is but one Master for all of us, Christ Jesus, to whom you ought to conform yourself in all things. No one ought to follow His enactments more closely than you, as Christ will hold you doubly responsible. Consider not what you command as right and just but rather command only what is right. Avoid those things that you can excuse in the common people. Whatever among them may be considered a minor infraction of law, consider in your case to be a crime of major proportions. Whatever honor, reverence, and dignity comes your way from your subjects should come from personal integrity rather than from your wealth. How many crimes are induced among your subjects just because of a fascination for wealth and pleasurable living that they see reflected among the well-to-do? You should set the example for them by never appearing with too great a display of wealth and expensive living. Let them learn after your example to despise such things and to honor virtue and temperance. You will not despise their poverty if you realize that you both have been redeemed with the same price.

In your defense against contempt and ambition place your reliance on good example rather than on the weapons of your guards. Let your rule of government be determined by the common good. The common people owe many things to you, but you in turn owe everything to them. In the face of ambition, refer all to Christ. Let offenses against your person be considered as trifles. Let no man's injury infuriate you unless he acted against you as a private person. If you are talented in affairs of state and courageous in danger, be mindful not of these talents but of the responsibilities you carry. And in your governing let your guide be Christ rather than your predecessor in office! If you must imitate great rulers from the past, imitate only those virtues which in them are in agreement with the virtues of Christ. Let no empire be to you of such worth that you would deviate from justice for its sake. Christ will more than reward you for the loss of such an empire. Nothing is more admirable in rulers than their imitation of Christ. He was great in that He hid the secret of His kingdom here on earth. He denied that His kingdom was of this world, although He was in reality the king of heaven and earth.

It is always a source of amazement to me that popes and

bishops so indiscreetly wish to be called lords and masters when Christ forbade His disciples to be called either. We must ever bear in mind that there is but one Lord and Master, Christ Jesus, our Head. The expressions apostle, shepherd, bishop, are terms denoting office or service, not dominion or rule. Pope, abbot, are terms meaning love, not power. Yet we are living in a world that has grown alien to the world of Christ both in doctrine and practice. There are too many who think that the expression "world" refers only to those who have embraced the monastic state. In the Gospel, for the Apostles, and for Augustine, Ambrose, and Jerome, the expression means the infidel, enemies of the faith and of the Cross of Christ. It consists of all those who place their care in tomorrow, who strive after riches and sensible pleasures. This world has not known Christ who is the true light of the world. It was from this world that Christ separated, not only His Apostles, but all men who would be worthy of Him. How then can we say that this world, everywhere condemned in Scripture, should be associated with Christendom and in its name flatter and maintain our own vices?

Too many of our theologians and teachers only make this matter worse by adapting the words of Scripture to the justification of their own crimes. In truth Scripture should be a source of that norm of behavior that can correct them. Too often do rulers today, reading that all power is from God, justify the perpetration of most horrible crimes. How many do not try to establish a new order of charity that engenders a greater regard for their own possessions than for their neighbor's, that sets their own life and fame over all others? Men will not defend the good name of their neighbor if by doing so they in any way tarnish their own. Who will not forsake their neighbor in time of danger, in order to save themselves? Pointing to the fact that many great saints were also great sinners is hardly a commendable thing. Peter out of fear of death denied Christ, yet he willingly died for Him later on. Do you think this is sufficient reason to deny Christ on so many occasions? Paul sinned in persecuting Christ, but once he was aware of this he immediately changed his ways. Matthew was summoned but once and he immediately abandoned his position as a tax collector to follow Christ. It is indeed a sad state of affairs when we have given to vices the names of virtues, when we are more diligent in defending our vices than in correcting them, and when we even turn to Scripture to condone them. You have imitated David and Mary Magdalene as sinners; imitate them, also, in their repentance and love of God.

Keep all this in mind, my brother in Christ, and accept this advice: Have only contempt for the changeable crowd with its ways. To be holy, ignore the demands of your senses. Embrace Christianity with your whole heart. Adapt your personality to the men you deal with so that your inner heart may not lose its strength of resolution. Be friendly and affable, courteous and pleasant to these men so that no harshness of yours might keep them from Christ. Express your feelings with actions, not with angry words. Do not fear the crowd to the extent that you dare not defend the truth. Action of a humane kind ought to improve relations between men, and not lead to deception.

### Seventh Rule.

We are weak human beings and cannot attain fully to these ideals. This does not mean that we should stop trying but, on the contrary, it means that we should come as close to them as we possibly can. The way to happiness is a rapid one, because all we have to do is turn our minds to things spiritual. Once this is done the love of Christ and things of the spirit will follow in exactly the same way as the shadow follows the body when the sun appears. The further you advance with your loving of Christ, the higher you will be able to rise above the transitory things of the world. The more you look to interior, spiritual things the less exterior, material things will attract you. Follow the example of the scholar seeking natural knowledge: he never lets any setback stop him in his quest.

To stay free from vice we have to be prudent. A person

convalescing is closer to true health when the causes of his sickness are taken away. A soul is the same way: remove it from the habit of sinning and it will be more capable of receiving God's grace, even though it is not perfect yet. If the example of the saints is too much for us, we should at least have enough pride not to let ourselves be outdistanced by pagans. With little knowledge of God and less of hell many of them have managed to lead clean and upright lives. Some of them even suffered loss of property and of life for this. If your hopes of heaven or your fears of hell fail you, try to let your natural disgust for sin motivate you. Youths especially should be taught to learn about sin from the opinions of the informed rather than to say foolishly that they will learn what sin is from their own experience. If they follow the latter course they will ruin their lives before they know what life is.

Avoid sin for the simple reason that Christ loves you. But if you cannot do this, try to avoid it merely for your own sake, because the possession of natural virtue, at least, is better than complete immorality. Furthermore, natural virtues form a good base from which to rise to higher spiritual things.

### Eighth Rule.

If you have frequent and heavy temptations do not begin to worry that God feels you are not good enough for Him. Think of it this way: He is a loving father teaching a future heir or punishing a beloved son. Or He is a lonely man searching out a friend. Begin to worry when you do *not* have temptation, because that is a sure sign that you are outside the pale of mercy. Job, who was God's friend; the Church fathers — Jerome, Benedict, Francis; all had terrible temptations. Follow their lead; let them help you. Be consoled that suffering is common to many great men. Try all the harder because when you conquer you will be in their company. "God will not forsake you, and will not let you be tempted more than you are able to bear."

### Ninth Rule.

Careful generals set guards even in times of peace. You should be like a general and always look for the next assault of the enemy. "For he ever goes about seeking whom he may destroy." Prepare yourself for his attack and repulse him when he comes. Remember that evil is never either easily or totally conquered. Before the children of Babylon grow up, dash them on the rock that is Christ.

### Tenth Rule.

Here are some suggestions for handling temptation: Make a violent effort to put sinful thoughts out of your mind. Turn around and spit, as it were, in the face of the tempter. Or fasten your attention on some holy task and apply all your powers of concentration to it. Or pray with all your might. You might have some particularly stirring passages from the Bible ready to use to encourage yourself in time of particularly painful mental agony.

### Eleventh Rule.

You have two dangers to face. One is giving in, the other is becoming proud after a temptation has been conquered. To be always safe from temptation, remember that Christ will help His followers do all things, because He says to them: "Have confidence; I have overcome the world." After temptation has passed you, or while you are performing some worthy task, give all the credit to God's kindness. If you allow yourself to feel that you have done this on your own ability and merit, your mind, the inner shrine, will become filled with prideful pleasure. Keep yourself in check by remembering St. Paul's words: "What do you have that you did not receive? And if you received why do you boast, as if you had not received it?"

There is, then, a double remedy for the double danger. During temptation have distrust of your own abilities and ask God's help. Place all hope of victory in His benevolent kindness. After temptation, remember your own unworthiness and immediately thank God.

### Twelfth Rule.

It is not sufficient for a soldier merely to repel an attack; he must also seize his attacker's weapons and turn them against him. Follow the example of the soldier and use temptation as a means to virtue. If your inclinations are to be greedy and selfish, increase your donations to charity. If you tend towards boasting, make a deliberate effort to be humble in all things. This way you can find in temptation a renewed determination to increase in piety. This procedure is the one that most galls Satan. It makes him afraid to tempt you because nothing is more hateful to the Author of Evil than that he should be responsible for some good.

### Thirteenth Rule.

Treat each battle as thought it were your last, and you will finish, in the end, victorious. It is possible that God in His kindness might reward you for your virtue by freeing you from temptation. It has happened before. Origen is an authority to be respected, and he believed that when a Christian is victorious the enemy's forces are lessened, and that once a Christian strongly defeats Satan God will not again permit him to be molested. In temptation, then, train your mind on the hope of eternal peace. But when you conquer a temptation think that the next one might come in the winking of an eye, and another immediately following that. As long as we fight in the garrison of the body, we should never put down our arms, never give up our post, never slacken our guard. We should always keep at heart the prophetic words: "I shall stand upon my watch."

### Fourteenth Rule.

We should not make the mistake of assuming that if we practice most of the virtues it will then be permissible to have one or two small vices. The enemy you ignore the most usually is the one who conquers. I find that many people fool themselves this way. They think that as far as their standards are concerned it is perfectly all right to practice one or two of the lesser vices and be the last person to commit one of the remaining ones. Most of those whom people call good certainly would be the last to commit theft, or homicide, or adultery, or rape, or incest. Yet they might not be above an occasional fornication or some other pleasure. Or these same "good" people might from time to time overindulge, or use vile language, or boast. Now really, if one vice can fool us this way, why cannot the other ones? It is not that these "good" people permit themselves one vice and have all the other virtues, but rather that these "virtues" are really only virtuous-seeming habits which their personality or education has imparted to them. If a person, like a true Christian, detests one vice he must, like a true Christian, detest all of them. If a person has true charity he holds all the vices in equal abomination, and does not let himself be fooled by any one of them, because he knows that the least of vices leads to the worst and that his negligence towards these least ones will lead him to destruction. It is impossible to root out all your bad habits at one time. But, still, you ought to try each day to work on one bad habit and replace it with a good one.

### Fifteenth Rule.

If you are afraid of what you go through in overcoming a temptation, think along these lines. Do *not* compare the difficulties of combating temptation with the pleasures of the sin.

*Do* compare the bitterness of the fight with the bitterness which sin brings. Before a sin is committed the guilt in which the sin results has a sweet and comfortable air about it. But think of the sweetness and comfort which will come to you when you have won out, and you will have little difficulty making the choice.

Those who are not careful enough are fooled because they compare the difficulties of overcoming temptation with the pleasure of the sin. They pay no attention to the consequences of either. The man who gave in will be worse off than the man who did not, because during the next trial his difficulty will be much harder to bear than that of the man who did not give in. The victor's pleasure will be far greater and longer lasting than the sinner's pleasure. The man who carefully weighs both alternatives will see this easily. Every Christian should realize what follows when he overcomes temptation, and the more he does this, the more will his victory mean to him.

If you should be wounded when the enemy unexpectedly attacks, do not give in. Many weak-willed and effeminate persons give up completely if they have been beaten once. They quit fighting, allow complete immorality to overcome them, and never even think of trying to regain their liberty. This faint-heartedness is dangerous, and although it is not identified with hopelessness itself, it usually leads to despair, which is the most desperate of sins. A good soldier never admits defeat, even when he is in retreat. Imitate the soldier, and do not despair if you have fallen into sin. The good soldier's temporary defeat and painful wounds seldom drive him from the field. They spur him to gather his strength and fight harder than before. We must be the same way. If spiritual disaster strikes us we should quickly renew our courage. When sin disgraces us we should find new resolution, new eagerness to live again a life of virtue. One wound is easier to take care of than many wounds; a recent wound is easier to heal than an infected one. Keep in mind and take courage from Demosthenes: "A fleeing man will fight again." The prophet David, Solomon the King, Peter the first pope, the Apostle Paul — all of these men sinned. Perhaps God let them sin so that you could follow their example and not despair. Stand up on your own two feet, and do it quickly and courageously. Return to the fight with fire in your heart. Control and caution are the watchwords. A pious man who overcomes great sin is all the more pious. What makes a man evil is not that he sins but that he *loves* his sin.

### Seventeenth Rule.

Each temptation has its own appropriate remedy. There is, however, one remedy which can be applied to any and all temptations, and that is the Cross, which is the example for those who fall, the refuge for those who toil, and the weapon for those in the fray. This is the one weapon you should use against the devil. The people have the Passion read to them, and adore the image of the Cross. They strengthen themselves by hanging crosses about themselves and by keeping parts of the true Cross about their homes. They work themselves into veritable agonies as they meditate on Christ's Passion, and cry tears of compassion for Him. This is all well and good for the ignorant. The true value of the Cross, however, is in profiting from its many examples. You cannot say that a person loves Christ if he does not follow His example.

If you want to meditate successfully on the Cross, you must have a plan of action, realizing that you are fighting a life-and-death battle. Everything should be carefully figured out, so that when the time comes for you to make use of your plan you will know exactly what to do. You must match the various parts of the Passion with the particular vices you are afflicted with and want to be rid of. There is no temptation or vice for which Christ did not furnish a remedy on the Cross. For example, when ambition pushes you to want to be great in the eyes of men, think, my suffering brother, of how great Christ is, and to what extent He lowered Himself to atone for your sins.

When envy fills your mind, remember how gently and sincerely He poured Himself out for our benefit. He was good to the very worst of us. When gluttony is the problem, think of how He drank vinegar and gall. When lust tempts you, remember how Christ lived. All His life He denied Himself these pleasures and suffered discomfort, punishment, and misfortune. He will assist you, too, when anger burns inside of you. Think of how He stood like a lamb, silent before His shearers.

If poverty or avarice are your temptations, remember that God owns all things and that for your sake He became so poor that He did not even have a place to rest His head. If you follow this plan it will not be painful to resist temptation. It may even be easy because you will know that you have conformed yourself to your Leader, and even given, in a roundabout way, thanks to Him for the agony which He endured for you.

### Eighteenth Rule.

If we recall, when passion stirs us to commit sin, how loathsome, abominable, and detestable sin is, this will help to counteract the temptation. For those whose spiritual life is moderately comfortable this is the most effective remedy. It will also be of some help to those who are not so spiritually well-off. We worry and scheme about trifling matters of no real importance. Before we sign up with the Devil by committing sin should we not stop to consider our own worth as humans, seeing the terrible price that was paid for us? To consider that we, the most noble of God's creatures, were created for an end? That the marvels of the world were created for us? That we are of the company of the angels and heirs to immortality? That we are members of Christ's body, and members of the Church; that the Holy Spirit dwells in us and that we are made in the image and likeness of God? Then when we have weighed this side of the scale should we not consider how sin is a sickness of the body, mind, and soul? That sin is the serpent's poison; that when we sin we sign a contract to enslave ourselves to the Devil? Even in this age innocence cannot be willingly destroyed.

Having weighed both sides of the balance, ask yourself whether it is worthwhile to fall from such dignity for a pleasure which is gone in a second; to fall from such dignity into a trap where your own efforts to free yourself will be useless.

### Nineteenth Rule.

Compare the two opposing forces. You make God your enemy by sinning, and by sinning you set up for your master the Devil. Your innocence makes you God's friend, with the rank and privilege of a son. Your sin makes you a servant and son to the Devil. One is an eternal fountain, the Mount Ida of utter beauty and happiness. The other is the Father of Evil, of complete depravity, and of unutterable unhappiness. God does nothing but good for you; the Devil can only harm you.

God began your life by filling you with immeasurable goodness. He redeemed you with great mercy; He bestows riches on you with complete generosity. He helps you gently in your shortcomings; receives you joyfully when you come to your senses. But the Devil lays traps for you with perverse joy, bringing you nothing but misery. He tries every day to drag all of mankind down to the bottom of hell.

When you have considered all this, speak with yourself this way: Even forgetting where I come from and all that God has done for me, will I for the sake of a pleasure which will soon pass desert my noble, loving, and deserving parent and enslave myself to the most cruel of masters? Can I not be superior to the Devil, just as I am superior to a deformed dwarf? I will flee the Evil One who desires man's ruin.

### Twentieth Rule.

The rewards are as different as the givers. What can be

farther apart than everlasting death and everlasting life? What is more in contrast than the delightful companionship of the citizens of heaven and the horrible company of the damned? No Christian could have any difficulty in knowing which is better. He would have to be insane to make any mistake. The contrast is not only after death, but even during life. Virtue has its own reward, and once a person has it, he would not exchange it for anything in the world, because he has the peace of mind, the happiness, and heavenly joy of a pure conscience. The horrors of a troubled conscience are the worst consequence of all the things which come from sin. On the other hand, peace is the hundredfold Christ promised in the Gospel. Peace is the preview of eternal happiness that He gives to us. This is the wonderful gift that the Apostle spoke of when He said that "neither eye has seen nor ear heard, nor has it entered into the heart of man what God has prepared for those who love Him," even in time. The worm eats the wicked even in the world; they already carry the flames of hell with them. The unending agony that haunts the habitual sinner is nothing less than hell.

Virtue is worth seeking for itself. Each virtue has an opposing sin whose very causes should be avoided. Keep this in mind if you want to take part in the glories of heaven.

### Twenty-first Rule.

Life is sad and miserable, short and quick. Death lies in wait on every side, haunting us. Since we do not know when Death will come to us, how foolish it would be to continue living the kind of life which would damn us forever if we died unexpectedly.

### Twenty-second Rule.

The worst evil is hardness of heart. Those who do not repent, who deliberately remain in their habits of sin, have the most to fear. Careful thought about this will reveal how few there are who are truly converted from evil habits, especially among those who have prolonged their lives of sin right up to the end. The path down to evil is quick, slippery, and easy. But to turn and "to go forth to the upper air . . . this is effort, this is toil." Think of Aesop's goat before you descend and remember that climbing out is not easy.

### Special Remedies For Particular Vices.

So far we have been considering common remedies against vices in general. Now we will take up vices one at a time and point out particular means which you should use to fight them.

### Lust.

Let us first consider lust. This is the first evil that attacks us. Its temptations are the strongest of all; its influence is the greatest. Lust drags more individuals to hell than any other vice. When lust tempts you, fight immediately with these weapons: First of all, think of how rotten, how unclean, how utterly unworthy of human dignity lust is. It puts the divine in us on a level with the animals. We are destined to be with angels, to commune eternally with God. Remember how rotten and perverted, how momentary and fleeting, how pregnant with remorse and guilt lust is. Think of how we have already described the soul as noble and the body as beautiful. How twisted it is to defile for a swiftly passing pleasure the soul and the body. Christ consecrated with His own blood the body which lust desecrates and pollutes. It brings nothing but evil with it. No other vice brings bad reputation so fast and so quickly. It depletes and weakens the great gift handed down to us from our ancestors. It ruins mental alertness; destroys tact and consideration. It destroys the inclination to serious study and healthy pursuits and plunges one into the filth of moral degradation. It will deprive you of intelligence, no matter how great, and reason, no matter how sound. It drives youths out of their minds and forces wild lies into their mouths; it makes old age filthy and detestable. You will find that almost any evil you can think of has its roots in lust. Look what lust has done to people you know. It destroys health; brings on disease. It ruins youth before its time, and speeds the coming of a horrible old age.

Think of all the young adults, of all the charming virgins who have remained pure, and they will motivate you in your struggle for purity. If you follow their example you will be just as strong as they; the circumstances of their temptation were much the same as yours. If they could do it, so can you. Think how honorable and pleasant a pure soul and body are. Purity in particular makes angels our friends and enables us to receive the Holy Spirit. There is no vice which the Holy Spirit loathes more than impurity. He is the lover of purity. Clean minds are the favorite abode of the Holy Spirit. Purity delights Him.

Think of the disgrace and madness which loving a prostitute brings. Think of the mental torture, the endless and lying protestations. There is nothing manly or virile about such a relationship. There is no love; it can only be termed an emotional aberration. Think of all the social evil that uncontrolled evil brings: mistreatment of parents, and friends, waste of wealth, rapine, murder, blasphemy, etc. Life is empty and fleeting, like a passing cloud. Death sets his trap without regard to where you are or what you are doing. Think of all your acquaintances and friends who died unexpectedly, especially those who used to be your partners in sin. The lightening-fast judgment that followed their unprovided deaths sent them to hell, and all for the fleeting pleasures of a passing moment. It is not such a big thing to resist impurity for the sake of Christ who suffered the Crucifixion for you. Will you crucify Him again with your illicit pleasures and put Him again to torture? At the same time He has literally heaped benefits and blessings on your soul, although you deserve absolutely nothing. You can never repay Him, but you could make a start by imitating His goodness and purity. When a temptation comes to you, think of your guardian angel. He protects you and witnesses everything that you do. Think of your God who sees even the most secret places of heaven and earth. Would you do in the presence of heaven's court what you would be ashamed to do in the presence of the lowest of human beings?

When temptation comes, think of your two alternatives. Either you will become so perverse and your mind so blind that impurity will become ingrained in you the rest of your life or, by God's grace, you will see what you are doing and with almost endless suffering you will manage to rid yourself of this evil. Avoid the temptation immediately and you will avoid these painful alternatives.

Let your state of life motivate you. If you are a priest, remember that you are consecrated to God. Could anything be worse than to touch the rotten, stinking flesh of a whore with your mouth that receives the Body and Blood of Christ, or to handle loathsome filth with the same hands that execute the most beautiful and incomprehensible mysteries? Where is the consistency between oneness in body and soul with God and oneness in body with a whore? If you have a good education think how poor it is for you to share divine thoughts with thoughts worthy of shame and rebuke. If you are of the upper classes think of the example you give to others. If you are married, your marriage is the symbol of the union of Christ and His Church. If you are in the flower of youth nothing will pollute you faster, nothing will haunt your memory more than this stupidity. Nothing is more painful than the stings of a sinful pleasure once gone. For a woman nothing is more noble than her chastity, nothing more shameful than the loss of it. If you are old nothing is more monstrous, nothing more provocative of scornful laughter than impurity.

Here is a summary of suggestions that will save you from sins of the flesh. As fast as you can, flee from every occasion without exception. (This is good advice for *any* temptation. He who loves danger is likely to perish in it. The advice, however, is particularly good with regard to those sirens who cannot be avoided except in immediate flight.) Also, drink and eat with moderation. Be temperate even in pleasures that are allowed. Remember two things: that Christ died for you and that you will one day die. In view of these things, have only pure and reliable individuals for companions, avoid corrupt and lustful conversations like the plague, flee idleness and occupy your thoughts with serious contemplation of things eternal. Especially, dedicate your whole heart to study of the Scriptures and to frequent and pure prayer, particularly during temptation.

### *Avarice.*

If you feel that your nature tends toward avarice, or if the Devil tempts you with that sin, put the above rules into action and think of the greatness of your value as a human being, and of the end for which you were created and redeemed, because God wants you always to enjoy the highest good. The vast machine which is the earth was created to serve your ends. How narrow-minded and unthinking not to use it as a means but to be entranced with it as an end. This is man's error and is a stupid and worthless one. What are gold and silver but red and white earth? You are a disciple of Christ and are called to a far greater possession than that of gold. Even some of the pagan philosophers had only contempt for it. Forget gold and admire something truly great.

I am contradicted, however, by an argument full of vague generalities that even Christians use. Their only pleasure is in the deception of themselves. Their argument runs like this: "The more wealth one has, the easier one can take care of the necessities of life. One *must* lead a healthful existence, rear and educate one's children, be honored by one's fellow men. The more money the better. How can you live a good life any other way?" Nine out of ten Christians feel this way. They have cloaked their desire in necessity. Let me begin my answer by throwing back at them what Christ said about the lilies and the birds living each day and what He said about emulating them. Let me say that the Apostles carried neither wallet nor moneybag. Let me say that Christ told us that, when we have forsaken all else, we should seek first the kingdom of heaven and all things will be added unto us. A person who strives to be godly will always have enough to get along. We really do not require very much. What we often do, though, is to set a limit on what we require on a basis of our own covetousness.

I am not greatly impressed with those who with one vow dispossess themselves of everything they have and then run around for the rest of their lives begging shamelessly. It is not wrong to have money. It only becomes wrong when money is loved as an end instead of looked on as a means. If you should become rich, act like the generous steward; if you should become poor do not feel robbed, but rather feel as though a friend had relieved you of a dangerous thing. A person who spends his whole life gathering wealth might be a good businessman but he can hardly be a good Christian. His very preoccupation with wealth betrays a lack of trust in Christ who so liberally provides for the birds of the air.

Wealth is supposed to bring with it many good things. (Epictetus puts it lowest on the scale of things to be desired.) What does wealth contribute to your intelligence? You cannot say it brings wisdom or intelligence or understanding. Or that it brings health or beauty. You might say it brings honor. But I ask what kind of honor and reputation it brings. True honor can only come from Christ; it is a reward for virtue and not for money. If your *mental* poverty were exposed you certainly would not be honored. No one can say a wealthy person has true friendship; the vast majority of his "friends" want his money and can hardly wait until he dies.

What wealth really brings is a host of evils. That is why Christ compares wealth to thorns that rip and tear all peace and quietness with a thousand never-ending cares. He tells us that it is easier for a camel to enter the eye of a needle than it is for a rich man to enter the kingdom of heaven. St. Jerome says that a rich man must be either dishonest himself or the heir of a dishonest man. You can neither keep nor get great riches without sin. Wealth robs one of a sense of value. St. Paul tells us that avarice and idolatry are the same things, while Christ says that we cannot serve God and Mammon at the same time.

### *Ambition.*

If your desire for things of this world ever becomes exaggerated, then following these suggestions will help you to put things in the proper perspective.

True honor is based upon virtue and upon nothing else but virtue. This comes from what we have said above and ought to be said before anything else. Even *true* honor is not an end in itself. Christ's example teaches us that Christians should go after only one kind of honor, that of being praised not by men but by God. The Apostle says: "He whom God commends is approved." If, for example, wicked men praise someone for something which is actually not true, this is not honor but a huge scandal. If honor comes for something shared by the honest and the dishonest — say beauty, wealth, strength, birth — that is not really honor either. No one is praised for doing dishonorable things. On the other hand, when one is praised for an honorable thing, this is honor. But people who deserve honor do not seek it but are content with the basic goodness of the act which brings the honor. You can see now how the honors which most people desire so avidly are really empty and ridiculous. Because, in the first place, honor is bestowed by those who do not distinguish between honesty and dishonesty. In the second place, it is usually bestowed for actions of dubious goodness, and sometimes even for bad actions. And, in the third place, it is usually given to an undeserving person.

Honor is bestowed for a number of reasons. Some people do it from fear. These people themselves are to be feared. Some do it so you can enjoy what they say to you. In this case you are being made fun of. Others bestow praise because they admire nothing, consider nothing honorable. These are to be pitied. Perhaps a sincere person will judge you to be truly worthy of honor. If he is not right about you, try to change yourself to live up to his expectations. If he is right about you, remember that God, not you, is responsible for your honorable traits. If you want to avoid honor that is false, avoid virtue that is false. Besides, what could be more stupid than to judge yourself by others' opinions of you? You know how changeable people are. They give you honor one minute and take it away the next. Nothing is more foolish than becoming proud of honor when you earn it or becoming angry when you lose it. Honor falls as often as not on unworthy people. How can honor have truth to it when people worse than you share the honor?

How peaceful is the calm of a modest and private life as compared to the lives of those powerful people always in the public eye. How difficult for the celebrity to keep his two feet on the ground and not fall on the slippery path. How difficult to keep perspective. The higher the pedestal, the more devastating the fall. Every honor brings responsibility with it. God's judgment will fall more severely on those who grab in all directions for honor, knocking everyone else out of the way. His mercy comes more easily to those who realize their weaknesses. Those who set themselves apart to receive honor from men also set themselves apart from the men who receive God's special graces. Follow Christ's example. According to the way men think, who was ever more despised and lower than Christ? He fled every honor offered Him — He was above honor. He accepted scorn riding on an ass. Recall to yourself the robe and the crown of thorns and how He was condemned. Recall the horrible way He chose to die. He scorned the world *but* He was glorified by the Father. Christ's Cross will be your salvation — let the Cross be your honor. What good are honors if angels curse you and God looks in the other direction when you pass?

### Pride and Haughtiness.

Not to be a proud and haughty person, you have to follow the old proverb and "know thyself." That is to say, you must regard your special talents, whatever beauty or fame you have, as gifts from God, and not as things you earned for yourself. Whatever is low and mean is not God's doing, however. Here you can only blame yourself. Remember the squalor of your birth and how naked and poor you were when you crawled into the light of day like a little animal. Just think of all the disease and misfortune you were exposed to as a child. Little things could make you deathly ill.

Self-praise is ridiculous. If you flatter yourself for some inconsequential thing, you are foolish; if for some wicked thing, you are mad. And if you praise yourself for a good thing, you are ungrateful. Nothing is more stupid and unwise than to flatter oneself. Even if you are in a position to do what you will, your tendencies toward pride will be checked by recalling how great and powerful God is, how He could break you in two by snapping His fingers. If He levels the hills and did not spare the angels, will He allow *you* to raise your head in pride?

Comparing yourself to those better than you will also help you. If you think you are handsome, compare yourself to someone better looking than yourself. If you feel you can teach well, think of those whom you know you have taught nothing. Do not think of all the wonderful things you are, but rather of all the wonderful things you are not, and St. Paul's words will have meaning for you, too: "forgetting those things which are behind, press toward those things which remain in front."

When pride tempts you, bring to mind those elements of your personality or behavior which embarrass you. Concentrate on your own obvious deficiencies. Never forget that pride was the vice Christ denounced the most and that, even among men, pride and arrogance meet with nothing but derision. A humble and gentle nature obtains not only God's favor but the goodwill and respect of your fellow man.

Briefly then, these two considerations will help you overcome pride: a realization of your own nothingness and a realization of the reward Christ has prepared for you.

### Anger and Revenge.

When resentment goads you to revenge, remember that anger is a false imitation of fortitude, and fortitude is the antithesis of anger. Nothing manifests a weaker will, nothing requires a feebler and weaker mind, than enjoyment of revenge. In trying to appear brave by not allowing an injury to go unpunished, a person displays only immaturity, since he cannot control his mind in a particular situation. It is noble and generous to ignore someone else's mistakes and quite the opposite to imitate them. The more a person has done harm, the more violent and insulting he is — in short, the more wicked he is — the more should you be careful not to imitate him. To avenge someone else's corruption brings only self-corruption. If you are not a person given to violence, all the world will know that you have been unjustly injured. But if you are revengeful, you only offer reasons to be treated in the same way. An injury inflicted is not lessened, but only increased by revenge. There will be no end to mutual injury if revenge is reciprocated between the two injured parties. Enemies increase on both sides, the pain can only grow more severe. And the more ingrained the habit of revenge, the more difficult it is to stop. A gentle and tolerant nature sometimes even influences the wrongdoer and makes a good friend out of an enemy. Vengeance usually brings only an increase of harm.

If you bear in mind the scale of values we have worked out, you will remember that only the outer man can be harmed by other men. God alone can take away the worthwhile things of the inner man, and He usually does this only to unkind men.

The only person that can harm a Christian is himself, and no injuries bring as much pain as self-inflicted ones. If you will use your intelligence concerning injuries you will not make too much of them; you will also lessen their gravity by considering mitigating circumstances. You may have been injured, but you may also know it will soon be made up for. Or perhaps the person who did it was only a child, or an inexperienced youth; maybe the person acted on someone else's advice, or maybe he acted with no previous reflection at all. He might have been drunk at the time. He is therefore to be forgiven. If the person is a member of your family or a close friend, he deserves to be forgiven because you love him or because you respect his authority. If the person has done you a number of good turns, take that fact into consideration. A liberal mind will not remember only the injuries and forget all the good things a person may have done. Lastly, when you fight your revengeful tendencies, think of how many times you have offended God. God will not forget the law He established, "to forgive us our trespasses as we forgive those who trespass against us."

You could rush off to Rome or Compostela and buy up a million indulgences, but in the last analysis there is no better way of reconciling yourself with God than reconciling yourself with your brother. It is really impossible to be seriously sinned against by your fellow man. Pardon your neighbor his offenses, so that Christ might forgive you your countless thousands of sins. It is difficult, you say, to forgive when you are carried away with anger. Just remember what Christ suffered for you — remember the patience with which He allowed Himself to be insulted, chained, lashed, executed. And you were once nothing more than His enemy. Even now the infinitely gentle Christ tolerates you and your daily repetition of sins. Do not boast of the Head and refuse to take care of the Body. You will not be one of Christ's members unless you follow in His footsteps. The only praiseworthy anger is against vice, not against man.

How can you expect mercy for yourself and still be so unjust to your brother? Is it so much to expect you to forgive a sinner when Christ Himself prayed to His Father for those who crucified Him? Is it so difficult to be told not to strike back at the brother whom you are commanded to love? Are you really qualified to punish someone who hurts you? Let pity and not a desire to punish motivate you in your dealing with those who have harmed you. Be angry at the man's vice and not at the man himself. If your personality gives you a tendency towards anger, then prepare yourself for every contingency by repeating to yourself that you are determined to do or say nothing while you are angered. When you make a decision in anger, hold off putting it into effect until your anger subsides — even if it is a just decision. There is no difference between a person who has lost control of his mind and one who is unduly angered. Remember how often in the past you have regretted something you did or said in anger. Why not let reason, or pity, or at least Christ, obtain what will come to pass anyhow. To overcome evil with goodness, malice with kindness, is to imitate Christ's perfect charity.

My dear friend, you can see what an immense number of vices we still have to discuss in a similar fashion. But we will leave what remains to your own skill. When we started it was not our intention to dissuade you from sin with an exhortation against each and every vice. All we wanted to do was to familiarize you with this new method of warfare so that you would be better prepared to defend yourself against the attacks of temptation which stem from your past life. Thus, we picked selected examples to show you how to act in particular instances, especially those to which we know your habits or personality incline. We described certain general rules which you should fix in your mind and use to counteract temptation. To keep them effective, go over them frequently and renew often your resolutions against such sins as detraction, slander, envy, gluttony, etc. These are the Christian soldier's only enemies. Against them he should fortify his mind in advance, using prayers, the sayings of the wise, the teachings in Scripture, and the examples of holy men, especially of Christ.

## Conclusion.

Even if I had been sure reading Scripture were going to supply you with all the spiritual advice you need, my love for you as a brother would have prompted me to write this extemporaneous treatise to help you with your pious plans to improve yourself. I wrote this all the more speedily because I was afraid you might fall into the clutches of those superstitious religious who, partly for their own advantage, partly out of great fervor, but certainly not according to any definite knowledge, "wander about seas and deserts." If they ever get their hands on a man returning from vices to virtue, then by outrageous arguments, blandishments, even threats, they try to drag him into the monastic life, as if one were not a Christian without a cowl. They fill up his heart with unsolvable worries and his conscience with innumerable scruples, truss him up with a lot of meaningless human traditions, and finally drive the poor wretch into a sort of Judaism where he is taught not to live but to fear.

Monasticism is not holiness, but a kind of life that can be useful or useless depending on a person's temperament and disposition. I neither recommend it nor do I condemn it. Let me warn you about it, however. Do not let your relationship with God depend on food, or on a particular form of worship, or on any visible thing, but only on those things we have already gone over. Whatever things you find Christ's image in, join yourself to them. If people do not think along lines which would make you better, withdraw yourself as much as possible from human companionship and take for companions Christ and His prophets and apostles.

Make yourself completely familiar with Paul. Keep him in your heart at all times; "day and night he should dwell in your hand." Memorize what he has to say. It has taken a long time and many a battle to come to these opinions. It is perhaps a presumptuous thing to do. Nevertheless, we rely on God's assistance and carefully devote our attention to it. After Origen,

Ambrose, Augustine, and so many more modern interpreters, we certainly shall not be alone in the task, and following them we do not think that our effort will be entirely fruitless.

There are certain detractors who think that true religion has nothing to do with good literature. Let me say that I have been studying the classics since my youth. For me a knowledge of Greek and Latin required many a long hard hour. I did not undertake this merely for the sake of empty fame, or for the childish pleasures of the mind. My sole purpose was that, knowing these writings, I might the better adorn the Lord's temple with literary richness. Too many in recent years, through their ignorance and boorishness, have been doing the very opposite. Through this type of study a person's naturally generous qualities can be kindled to a love of the Holy Scripture. I have, however, set this work of translating the Fathers apart for a few days so that I could write this for you, and point out for you a short cut, as it were, to Christ. I pray that Jesus will bless your undertaking and that He will favor your whole project. I pray also that He will multiply and increase the grace He has already given you in helping you with your transformation. My purpose is that you may quickly grow great in Him, and may hasten to a perfect manhood. In Him I bid you farewell, my brother and friend, who are ever beloved to my soul, and who are now dearer than before, and more pleasing.

*At the town of Saint Omer,*
*the year of Christ's birth, 1501.*

# Date Due

| | | |
|---|---|---|
| De 31 62 | AP 1 3 '85 | |
| MY 18 '64 | | |
| UY 15 '65 | NO 1 '85 | |
| AG 4 '65 | | |
| De 18 '65 | | |
| AP 18 '66 | | |
| MY 10 '66 | | |
| AP 26 '67 | | |
| | | |
| MY 1 69U | | |
| AP 22 70 | | |
| AP 11 72 | | |
| MY 4 72 | | |
| | | |
| | | |

Demco 293-5